D1644505

Acknowledgements

The people who have helped me in the production of this book are legion.

First on the list must be Alan Phillips, of G.M.C. Publications who, with Bernard Cooper, originally encouraged me to write for the house magazine, 'Woodworking Crafts'. Other G.M.C. stalwarts are John Haywood, who is the librarian, technical editor and the Lord knows what-all, and Sue Cleeve, who took on the editorship of this book.

I must also thank the many students who have attended my instruction courses. Their questions and the problems which they encountered really made me think again about my own techniques. Thanks must also go to the numerous people who have watched and asked questions of me at craft fairs, demonstrations etc. My fellow professional woodturners are a constant source of inspiration through their own writings and demonstrations . . . not that they have always been right!

Most of the photographs in the book were taken by Julian Powell, whom I almost drove insane with some of my layman's requests. Keep taking the tablets, Julian.

I thank Coronet Lathe and Tool Company Ltd., and Robert Sorby Ltd., for permission to use some of their illustrations.

Finally, I must say a big thank you to the Dixon family – particularly Sue, who undertook to decipher my illegible pencil scrawl and put it into a format which all, including myself, could read.

Metric Conversion Table
INCHES – MM

Inches		MM		Inches		MM		Inches		MM
¼″	—	6 mm		6″	—	150 mm		26″	—	660 mm
⅜″	—	10 mm		6⅛″	—	155 mm		27″	—	685 mm
½″	—	12 mm		6¼″	—	160 mm		28″	—	710 mm
⅝″	—	15 mm		6½″	—	165 mm		29″	—	735 mm
¾″	—	20 mm		6¾″	—	170 mm		30″	—	760 mm
⅞″	—	22 mm		7″ Fibre discs only		178 mm		31″	—	785 mm
1″	—	25 mm		7″	—	180 mm		32″	—	815 mm
1⅛″	—	30 mm		7¼″	—	185 mm		33″	—	840 mm
1¼″	—	32 mm		7½″	—	190 mm		34″	—	865 mm
1⅜″	—	35 mm		7¾″	—	195 mm		35″	—	890 mm
1½″	—	38 mm		8″	—	200 mm		36″	—	915 mm
1⅝″	—	40 mm		8¼″	—	210 mm		37″	—	940 mm
1¾″	—	45 mm		8½″	—	215 mm		38″	—	965 mm
2″	—	50 mm		8¾″	—	220 mm		39″	—	990 mm
2⅛″-2¼″	—	55 mm		9″	—	230 mm		40″	—	1015 mm
2⅜″	—	60 mm		9¼″	—	235 mm		41″	—	1040 mm
2½″	—	63 mm		9½″	—	240 mm		42″	—	1065 mm
2⅝″	—	65 mm		9¾″	—	250 mm		43″	—	1090 mm
2¾″	—	70 mm		10″	—	255 mm		44″	—	1120 mm
3″	—	75 mm		10⅛″	—	257 mm		45″	—	1145 mm
3⅛″	—	80 mm		11″	—	280 mm		46″	—	1170 mm
3¼″	—	85 mm		12″	—	305 mm		47″	—	1195 mm
3½″	—	90 mm		13″	—	330 mm		48″	—	1220 mm
3⅔″	—	93 mm		14″	—	355 mm		49″	—	1245 mm
3¾″	—	95 mm		15″	—	380 mm		50″	—	1270 mm
4″	—	100 mm		16″	—	405 mm		51″	—	1295 mm
4⅛″	—	105 mm		17″	—	430 mm		52″	—	1320 mm
4¼″-4⅜″	—	110 mm		18″	—	460 mm		53″	—	1345 mm
4½″	—	115 mm		19″	—	485 mm		54″	—	1370 mm
4¾″	—	120 mm		20″	—	510 mm		55″	—	1395 mm
5″	—	125 mm		21″	—	535 mm		56″	—	1420 mm
5⅛″	—	130 mm		22″	—	560 mm		57″	—	1450 mm
5¼″	—	135 mm		23″	—	585 mm		58″	—	1475 mm
5½″	—	140 mm		24″	—	610 mm		59″	—	1500 mm
5¾″	—	145 mm		25″	—	635 mm		60″	—	1525 mm

To obtain the metric size for dimensions under 60″, not shown in the above table, multiply the imperial size in inches by 25·4 and round to the nearest millimetre taking 0·5 mm upwards.

e.g. 9⅛″ × 25·4 = 231·8
= 232 mm

To obtain the metric size for dimensions over 60″ multiply the imperial size in inches by 25·4 and round up to the nearest 10 mm taking 5 mm upwards.

e.g. 67″ × 25·4 = 1701·8
= 1700 mm

Contents

Foreword

The universal appeal of creating things by hand attracts people from all walks of life to woodturning. As a hobby, it possesses magical properties of transport, relaxation and inspiration. As a commercial turner, every time I handle an interesting or exotic wood, I cannot fail but wonder at the journey it took to reach my workshop.

For many full-time woodturners, their craft began as a hobby. And, of the stars of the commercial trade, Reg Sherwin shines amongst the brightest.

I have known Reg for many years and have spent many happy hours in his company, talking about turning techniques and swapping experiences. I know, from talking to him, that his expertise is self-taught. Initially he was inspired and guided by the writings of Geoff Peters, one of the most talented woodturning instructors of our generation. But Reg's expertise comes from hands-on experience. This is the measure of a true craftsman; his knowledge is not purely theoretical, he has learnt from his mistakes and tried different techniques to expand his knowledge.

As you proceed through the book you will appreciate how painstaking Reg has been to learn and improve his ability. His desire to excel and willingness to improvise has made him a true professional.

Reg cannot be accused of taking life too seriously. You do not need to be in his company for long to appreciate his love of life and original sense of humour. From the beginning Reg could not contain his wit and, because of this, and his straightforward style of presentation, I feel sure everyone who reads this book will not only learn a great deal about woodturning, but will also enjoy the reading experience.

I am creating a library at my woodturning studio to enable my students to study past techniques and projects. It also gives them the opportunity to evaluate certain books before purchase. This library, and any other with a woodturning section, would be incomplete without a copy of this book.

I am sure this is a book that both hobbyist and professional can enjoy and benefit from, and one to which I will refer often. I would like to thank Reg for this marvellous explanation of the techniques he uses.

Allan Batty,
Allan McNair Woodturning Studio

Introduction

This book is not aimed specifically at the new-comer to woodturning, as it doesn't go into basic skills in any great detail. There are a great number of books which start with basics and the beginner should consult the bibliography for more information. This book is intended more for the turner who has 'done a bit'.

Being a skilled craft practised by individuals often working in isolation, woodturning can be a contentious subject. What is right for one person is not necessarily right for another. And yet, neither is it necessarily wrong either. Some of the things which I advocate in these pages will be frowned upon, indeed have already been frowned upon, by fellow professional turners. But they work for me!

Whilst there is information for all skill levels, my intention is to try to cover some of the aspects of turning which other books miss out on.

'Pleasure and Profit from Woodturning' is based on my experiences over the last nineteen years as a 'jobbing' turner. That is, one who never knows what type of work is coming into the workshop next. Because the book is based upon my own experiences, I do not mention the wide range of lathes, chucks, tools etc., which are available to today's turners, but of which I have had no direct experience.

Indeed, such is the pace of development in these specialised fields at the moment, that much of what is written on the subject is out of date before it gets into the bookshops. For this reason, I have contained my comments to a restricted range of hardware. If these omissions have offended any manufacturer, I apologise.

Finally, I hope that you, the reader, get as much pleasure out of reading the book as I have had in writing it.

1 Workshop Layout

1·1 General

The workshop where I spend most of my working time should be light and airy rather than having the cluttered and claustrophobic appearance that some have had in the past.

The first workshop I had was right alongside a picturesque and well-used canal.

I wasted the surroundings. Instead of making things to put into the shop which occupied the ground floor, and which attracted passing traffic, I spent too much time admiring the view from the upper window. Windows in workshops are for letting light in, not looking out of.

Plenty of windows, not receiving dazzling direct sunlight and solid walls to which the lathe can be fixed and dampen any vibration from machinery, are primary considerations when setting up a workshop.

The ceiling should not be too high; there is no point in having a hot roof and cold feet. I find 8 – 9′ at the lowest point is comfortable.

The floor should be firm – again as an anti-vibration measure. My preference is for concrete or tiles, with duckboards which I can put down at whatever machine I am working on.

Many workshops have wooden floors, which can be somewhat springy due to the support which they get – or don't get – from the joists.

If the workshop floor is springy, then the lathe should be positioned at the most solid place – usually against a wall – rather than near the centre of the 'drum skin' floor.

The wall will also provide possible support for the bench.

One of the venues where I sometimes demonstrate is of the drum skin type, and it is not a place for lace bobbin production. Any movement within 30 feet of the lathe can literally lead to lost production if the more slender items break.

1·2 Workshop Size

If you are a professional turner selling your produce, then the workshop can't be too big, except that it has to be paid for, if not in rent then certainly in heating.

I have found that a workshop of 500 square feet is a bit on the small side, but then I have a number of machines and ought also to have a good working space around them. The size of the workshop depends really upon what is to go in it, what type of work it is to be used for – there are different aspects of turning, some of which need assembly space for the products – and whether it is to be used by one or more people.

When contemplating a new workshop set-up, it is very useful to draw out a scale floor plan of the workshop and also scale down the machinery which it must take, then arrange the machinery on the plan in a number of different layouts. This way the best scheme can be found for the intended work, without the embarrassment of having to re-position heavy machinery due to poor planning.

An indication on the machine plans of where the operator will stand, where saw blades are, what doors open which way, will help to lessen the chance of bad positioning. Once, from the security of my home office, I placed a very heavy and unfamiliar double-drum sanding machine up against a wall, and afterwards discovered that the machine had a forgotten access door which I had cleverly positioned against the wall.

1·3   Strip Lighting

Strip lighting is useful as a general light source but individual machines should have ordinary bulbs of whatever wattage is required, otherwise the machine user is likely to fall foul of the stroboscopic effect.

This can, at times, make revolving parts on machines seem to be standing still because the blade, block of wood or whatever, is revolving at a speed which is compatible to the frequency of the strip light illuminating it. This phenomenon can cause some embarrassment to an operator's fingers, particularly in a noisy workshop.

Whilst on the subject of electricity, I like to have plenty of 13 amp power points around the workshop, preferring twin outlets to singles. This avoids the possibility of having to use lots of extension leads and adaptors – both of which are fine in small doses, but can be lethal when found in abundance.

1·4   Heating

Workshop heating is an important consideration, particularly in the climate of the United Kingdom.

It does make sense to use solid fuel heating where possible. I have a stove which will burn either fossil fuels, offcuts or, if loaded with care, wood shavings.

I recently met a miniaturist who kept a year's supply of timber in a shoe box, so he had an electric fan heater to keep him warm. A mouse would have perished from cold if relying on the heat produced by his lathe waste!

It is a good idea, if possible, to have a heat source close to where most of the time will be spent in the workshop, i.e. the lathe.

I have also found that I get a lot of heat from the stove chimney and so its positioning is important. Advice should be sought on chimney installation etc., so as to avoid problems like a smoke-filled workshop because the fire won't draw, or a leaking roof where the expanding and contracting chimney defies any of the orthodox sealing methods.

Some stoves can be persuaded to burn shavings by packing the shavings tightly round a central tapered column – which has been turned – and then when the column is carefully removed a flue hole is left in the middle of the shavings. A fire at the base of this hole usually has the shavings glowing nicely before too long. A mixture of sawdust and shavings can also be used but they must be packed tightly, otherwise the flue hole collapses and the workshop occupants get kippered.

1·5   Waste Removal

I like a quick means of moving the shavings from the lathe, giving me more production time during the day, and allowing the shavings to be bagged quickly at the end of each day, batch of work or whatever. A temporary screen behind me collects most of the day's output of waste in a neat pile before it gets chance to lose itself amongst the other machines.

1·6   Tool Storage

It is also a good idea to keep small tools etc., out of the shavings. I was forever losing tools when I had people working for me. A search amongst the ashes of the shavings-consuming bonfire was usually rewarding, although the hammers and screwdrivers looked a little the worse for wear in their handle departments.

I don't like storing turning tools with the blades down, be they sitting on their cutting edges in a rack, suspended through a recessed rack or held in position with clips.

If the blade is a bit on the loose side it is likely to fall out of its handle, possibly taking part of the turner with it. Much better, in my view, to keep unused tools in a covered tray or drawer under a bench, with the handles all at the same end to protect searching fingers.

The tools in current use I keep in a rack on the lathe bench (see fig. 1).

1·7   Dust Extraction

I deal in more detail with this subject in the next chapter, but note that a small vacuum cleaner can be most useful – particularly one

which not only sucks but which can also have its blow controlled.

A length of 9mm bore copper tube, with an adaptor made up by your friendly neighbourhood woodturner is very useful for blowing dust out of motors, corners and other woodturners' crevices.

1·8 Factory Inspectors

I have seen some turners working on lathes with unguarded pulleys.

If the factory inspector saw that, it would result in knuckles being rapped. In fact, unguarded pulleys often lead to this painful condition anyway.

It is a good idea to contact the local factory inspector, particularly if you intend to employ or to allow public access to the workshop. The address will be found in the local telephone directory under Factory Inspectorate.

I can imagine a lot of readers shaking their

1 Tool, calliper and pencil rack

heads at the thought of making contact with what some consider to be the enemy, but surely it is better to find the inspector than to have him or her find you, particularly if they have followed up a lead from the local accident hospital.

1·9 First Aid Box

Any workshop should have a first aid box which is kept stocked with the usual plasters, bandages, antiseptic creams etc. and which is easy to open with one hand, should the other one be the cause of needing to open it.

I also like to keep a watchmaker's eyeglass and a pair of fine tweezers handy as well. I prefer to remove splinters straight away rather than risk a sharp reminder of their presence when working on a saw or some similarly dangerous machine.

2 Saws and Other Machinery

2·1 Bandsaws

As I have already said, I do have a number of machines apart from woodturning lathes.

Most turners need the back-up of a saw at least, and I think a good bandsaw is more versatile than a circular saw if space or cost restricts the turner to just one machine.

A bandsaw is more economical than a circular saw in that the waste is usually less, it having a narrower kerf than its circular counterpart. Also it can rip, cross-cut and produce discs, whereas a disc from a circular saw does tend to be time-consuming and irregular. Also bandsaws are better than circular saws for converting twisted timber, the blade being more able to accept sudden changes in cutting angles as the warped timber is moved over the machine table.

However, small bandsaws should be avoided if a wide range of turning is to be attempted. Be wary of manufacturers' photographs which show small bandsaws cutting 2″ and thicker boards. I don't know of any rule of thumb as to machine capacity, versatility and robustness but you can always ask around and see what other woodworkers are achieving on their machines.

My bandsaw is an old 30″ throat Sagar with a tilting table. (See fig. 2.) The machine takes a 16 ft blade. I find a ⅜″ wide blade with six teeth per inch works fine. No doubt the number of teeth and their configuration is important, if not critical, but I can even cut thin ply and hardboard down to ⅛″ thick provided I use a slow feed. I know that at least one tooth should be in contact with the work at all times, but I haven't got the time to change blades constantly and so I use a slower feed when cutting this thin stuff. I could also, of course, back the workpiece with some scrap board, effectively thickening the area to be cut.

2 The bandsaw

2·2 Circular Saws

I also have a circular saw with an 18″ blade from the same (now out of business) manufacturer. The circular saw needs a much wider kerf than the bandsaw, and is therefore not as economical when dealing with either expensive timbers or boards which have a low waste factor. For instance, with the bandsaw I can get two pieces of 2″ × 2″ from a $4^1/_{16}$″ board – an important consideration even though the ripping operation takes longer.

Whichever circular saw is chosen, it should have a rise and fall table or arbor, to control the depth of cut. A tilting arbor for mitre sawing is preferable to a tilting table, the timber being easier to control when sawing.

2·3 Combination Machines

The third most used saw is, in fact, a Coronet Major combination lathe.

The machine has a 10″ saw blade, 4½″ planer with thicknessing attachment and a morticer, which I use for drilling holes. (See fig. 3.)

3 Coronet Major combination machine

I don't often need planed timber which is wider than 4½″ and I would rather have the floor space than a machine which I would use once in a blue moon. Also, lots of my customers have planers and I am not averse to the occasional bartering of services.

If space allows, a number of independent machines can have advantages over a combination. Why buy a morticer-cum-belt-sander-cum-jigsaw-cum-spindle-moulder, if you don't want all of these facilities? With more than one person in the workshop the dangerous situation of two independent operations on the same machine can lead to accidents.

I am reasonably happy with my combination machine but that is because I am the only one using it.

2·4 Pillar Drill

I do have, and frequently use, a pillar drill.

Whilst a lot of drilling can be done on the lathe, indeed I sometimes prefer the lathe for this work, the pillar drill is usually the quicker machine for general purpose work. I shall go into drilling in more detail in chapter 10.

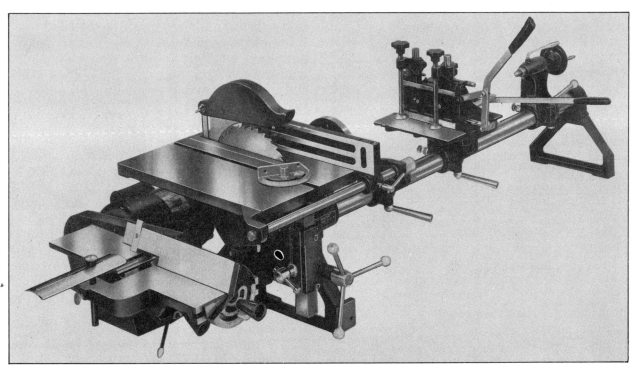

2·5   Grindstone

The last machine which is used by most wood-tuners is the grindstone.

Mine is a 6″ double-ended machine, although I do also have a 6″ grinding wheel on my demonstration lathe, a Coronet Minor.

My grinding wheels are ½″ wide and 60 grit. One of the wheels in the double-ended machine is the white aluminium oxide type, which is softer and generally used on high speed steel tools, having less tendency to burn the tool during grinding.

I have never used a whetstone for either shaping or sharpening tools, purely because of lack of space.

2·6   Linisher (or Belt Sander)

Some turners use a linisher, or belt sander, to sharpen tools, and I tried it for a while but found the grindstone more convenient. Also I use my linisher to sand wood and I don't want metal debris ingrained in the timber.

4 Linisher (or belt sander) and saw table

My 6″ linisher is, in fact, yet another attachment for the Major combination lathe but I have it rigged up on a floor-standing saw table. (See fig. 4.)

A plywood pulley takes the place of the saw-blade, the drive belt passing through the blade slot in the saw table and tension being adjusted by raising and lowering the privoted table.

When I decided to use this system of driving the linisher I spent a lot of time looking for a metal pulley which would fit the saw table arbor without success. Then I suddenly realised that I was a woodturner and had a piece of ply!

These then are the regularly used machines which support my hand turning lathes.

2·7   Ancillary Equipment

In addition, I have the following machines, also in support:

My engineering lathe, an old 'Acorn' (see fig. 5), is very useful for modifying, refurbishing and even sometimes making centres and other devices for the lathes.

I have no thread-cutting equipment for the Acorn and haven't needed to obtain any because if I need some device with a thread on it, I usually buy a nut or bolt with the appropriate thread and then machine the head.

I might even barter with my friendly neighbourhood engineer, who is also an amateur woodturner. It's not who you know that counts. Nor is it what you know. It is who you know and what *they* know.

Some time ago, I used to do a lot of work using 61″ square ply sheets ⅜″ thick and bought a portable cross-cut saw to convert these into more manageable sizes prior to presenting them to my machines. I use the saw rarely now, but should similar work come along again, the machine is waiting.

My last saw is a small 10″ electric chainsaw.

I pondered long and hard about buying a chainsaw, never having had the need for one. But then my attention was drawn to the offer of a free workmate folding bench if I bought the saw.

I already had a workmake and decided to accept the offer, sell the second bench and recover part of my outlay on the saw.

5 Engineering lathe

In fact I now use both benches more than the saw, but since I started making waney edge bowls a few years ago, the saw has come into its own, playing an important part in converting logs. I wouldn't now be without either the saw or the workmates.

I do have other machinery about the workshop, such as a power drill, an electric screwdriver, and a small, hand-held plunging router.

The vacuum cleaner already mentioned in chapter 1 is useful, but for the larger collection problems, an extractor is invaluable.

For some years I used a shop-made extractor called RIVEL. This stood for Reg's Incredible Vono Extraction Lash-up. (See fig. 6.) It worked just as well as a lot of better-looking models and cost me considerably less. I have now put RIVEL into retirement and bought a less-offensive looking device. RIVEL just would not have felt at home in my new workshop, which is open to public gaze.

2·8   Automatic Lathe

I do not have an automatic lathe at the moment, my interest being centred on hand turning and teaching, but if the right kind of enquiry comes up, then I would consider purchasing a suitable machine.

2·9   Use of Machines

So much for the machinery which I have. Now let's have a look at some of the lessons I have learned using it:

I am quite deliberately not giving basic instruction in machinery use as there are a lot of books which do that already. If you need such instructions then buy one of the books detailed in the bibliography, or go on a course of instruction, but above all, use your common sense.

I used to say to my operators, "These machines don't know the difference between beech and bone. They will chobble their way through anything which you may care to feed into them."

6 RIVEL (Reg's Incredible Vono Extraction Lash-up!)

2·10 Bandsaw Safety

First the bandsaw: When possible, I always work on the left of the blade, that is, between it and the machine frame.

There are two reasons for this. Firstly, if small pieces of wood are being sawn off as waste and they happen to get down the gap in the table into which the blade disappears, then they are on the outside of the blade and should fall clear. If they fall on the left hand side of the blade however, they could get trapped between it and the lower wheel, tightening the blade and thereby risking an accident.

Yes, I know that the slot in the throat plate should not be large enough to allow any waste to get where it shouldn't go. But slots wear.

The second reason for this left side approach is that in most of the blade breakages which I have witnessed (and it is not always possible to replace faulty blades before they convert themselves into double-ended and lethal metal ribbon) the blade breaks at, or just above, the point of entry on the workpiece. When the broken end manages to escape its guard it goes away from the frame and it tries to impale anything to the right of the slot, including hands.

If my approach to this subject leaves you a little green about the gills, well, better that than being red about the perforations!

2·11 Bandsawing Discs

I suspect that most people are aware of the pin method of producing discs from squares on a bandsaw. I have found it quicker to offer strips of timber up to the pin, making a number of discs from the same strip. (See fig. 7.) This method may seem a little laborious but is, in fact, quicker as it avoids an extra cross-cutting operation.

7 Bandsawing discs

2·12 Bandsaw Offcuts

I also suspend an offcuts sack on the right of the sawtable and save myself a sweeping up operation when I have a lot of bandsawing to do.

2·13   Cross-cutting

When cross-cutting timber, on either of the saws, I usually start from the newest end of the timber, it being the end which is least likely to have any seasoning splits in it.

If I am in any doubt as to the presence of splits I remove the first ½″ or so from the doubtful end, and if the waste comes away in a solid piece all is probably well. However, I still try to break the offcut, flexing it so as to stretch the new face and checking for cracks. (See fig. 8.) If it is solid then so should the other face be on the timber to be cut. If not, then take another cut and repeat the test.

8 Cracking up

9 Workmate outrigger

I do use carbide-tipped blades in the circular saws, as I am sure do most people now. They are well worth the extra cost, giving not only longer life but also better surface finishes as well.

When cross-cutting, on either of the saws, it is often possible to offer the timber to the saw more than one piece at a time. This does though, depend upon the size and length of the timber to be cut and the capacity of the machine which is cutting it.

Also, if you do cut in multiples, make sure that the strips on the bottom of the pile are being fed up to the fence as well as the top strip before the cut starts. It may sound a silly thing to say, but the next time I make that mistake won't be the first.

I have found that an elastic band will hold the free ends of a long bundle of dowels, both stopping them from splaying and also from slipping during this operation.

Multiple sawing however, is not to be undertaken if for some reason the job requires ultra-accuracy and squareness.

I find that long overhangs of timber can be supported when cross-cutting by using a workmate with a section of ply or blockboard edge down and gripped in it (see fig. 9). The top edge of the board should be smooth, polished and parallel to the top of the saw table.

3 Lathes

3·1 Introduction

There is no such thing as the perfect lathe.

If there was just one 'jobbing' woodturner in the world, then he or she would still not have the perfect lathe, although they could boast an enviable order book.

The reason that no lathe has reached the optimum in design is that there is such a wide variety of work which the turner can be asked to do. If a turner specialises in a particular type of work then the perfect lathe could be found. However, I tend to tackle any turning job which comes through the door.

I know of one machine which is considered to be the Rolls Royce of lathes for the bowl turner but which is decried by many spindle turners, myself included.

Whatever lathe you use, don't be reluctant to look at other makes and models which may add to your versatility.

3·2 Choice

I have for a number of years worked with the Coronet range of lathes, principally the Major but also the Minor, which has now been superseded by the Elf. I also have a No. 1 lathe from the same company.

I like the Coronet machines for a number of reasons. In no particular order, I list the three principal advantages of my choice of lathe.

Any lathe should be quiet running. I once spent half an hour in conversation with a well-known turner who was demonstrating at a woodworking show. We talked whilst the lathe was stationery but we shouted whilst it was running.

If I am going to spend all day in isolation with a working machine, I like to be able to listen to the radio as well.

The perennial problem with any lathe is that it usually has to cope with both spindle and bowl turning.

The bowl turner works best when he can stand in any position through at least 180° to the face of the job which he is working on. Outboard, swivelling head and sliding head lathes usually give this facility, depending upon situations within the workshop. Of course, pedestal mounted lathes with no long bed or tailstock to restrict the movement of either turner or tool would be the ultimate choice for the bowl turner.

Bowl working over the bed of the fixed head lathe can be a nuisance when the tool handles foul on the bed during cuts. Shorter handled tools can be used, certainly, but big bowls are better tackled with long handled tools, giving greater control to the turner.

Another advantage of the swivelling head lathe specifically, is that if the machine has to be used as a lathe/saw/planer combination, its position within the workshop is not quite so critical. I have had my swivelling head combination 'Major' near a door in a small workshop and when ripping or planing long stuff, the headstock was rotated so that the outfeed side pointed towards the open door. Just post a sentry to watch out for passing traffic, that's all.

The third advantage of my choice of lathe is the solid round bed on both the Major and Minor.

I have found when repetition turning that it is very useful to be able to swing the tool rest round the bed in a one-handed action, without the rest losing its angle in relation to the bed. This facility is most useful when the work has been roughed out and the tool rest is repositioned nearer the revolving wood for the detailed turning. The rest can also be pivoted away from the work for safe sanding.

I rarely use the keyway in the bed of the Major, which is just a location device anyway, preferring to work with the saddle key held back from engaging in the slot.

I do, of course, use the keyway when positioning the tailstock, although this is not always as critical as some people suggest. To prove the point, or more particularly, to confound critics of Coronet, I have sometimes off set the tailstock of my Minor by up to ten degrees and then turned a cylinder.

It is particularly useful to be able to swivel the tailstock out of the way with one hand as well, on some types of work. I have yet to suffer an attack of tailstock elbow, an occupational hazard with all but solid, single-round bed spindle lathes. Unfortunately, this one-handed facility is not available on all types of Major lathes, but mine are earlier models.

A disadvantage of my larger Major is that it allows only a 9" swing when working between centres. This means that a piece of 6" square timber can just be swung, provided the lathe saddles can be kept clear of the rotating corners. I have had a special driving centre made up to help here (see fig. 81, chapter 9·1).

Not all people would want to swing 6" square timber between centres, but I have occasionally been asked to do even larger sections and have had to say no. And that is something which the professional turner can't afford to say too often.

The second disadvantage of my chosen lathe is that when turning bowls, the bowl-turning bracket requires spanner adjustment. It can be both irritating and time-consuming to have to search for spanners if I am making a batch of bowls and need to make constant adjustments to the tool rest position.

The new Number 1 lathe, however, avoids this problem by utilising locking levers rather than spanners.

Choice of lathe then is often dictated by the type of work to be undertaken, or vice-versa.

For instance, to overcome the spanner adjustment problem with the Major and Minor lathes, I have recently bought a Harrison Graduate Short Bed lathe, specifically for bowl work. (See fig. 10.)

The ideal, I suppose, is to have one of every

10 *Graduate short bed, set up for inboard work*

lathe ever made, but think of the rent you would need for the workshop. The heating bill would be a bit on the uppish side as well!

3·3 Size of Lathe

One fallacy I would like to dispel is that small work must be done on a small lathe. My principal lathe has an extended bed and I can get 10 feet between centres (see fig. 11). I regularly use the same lathe for lace bobbins, and sometimes for quite small work.

I agree that the miniaturist only needs a small lathe, giving him greater control over the timber, faster cutting speeds and a requirement for less space. However, he has specialised, whereas I am talking about the jobbing turner.

11 Major with 10 foot centres

3·4   The Ideal Lathe

Any lathe should be quiet running, have a range of speeds from about 300 rpm to 2,500 rpm, allow easy speed change, have an externally-threaded head stock spindle to take today's range of chucks etc., have a morse taper in both head and tailstock, have facility for a two-post tool rest, safe switchgear (more of this in a moment), be robust and heavy, and give good capacity and accessibility in both spindle and bowl turning. Not a lot to ask for!

3·5   Switch Gear

I prefer lathes which have push button starters rather than switches. I also like the off button to be placed round about knee height, where it can be found with the leg if both hands are dealing with an emergency.

Cut-out buttons can usually be fitted to most lathes as an addition to the standard switchgear, should the starter be a fixture on the lathe. I shall soon have a cut-out at the tailstock end of my long bed lathe so that I can switch the machine off in a hurry without having to whistle for a taxi to take me to the starter box. And the button will, of course, be at knee height.

The lathe, and other machines come to that,

should have a cut-out device, so that if the power supply is interrupted for some reason, the machine is automatically switched off. This saves the possible embarrassment of a machine suddenly starting up again when the power is restored.

3·6   Second Hand Lathes

Second hand lathes are sometimes available but in my experience, good ones hold their price and so there are few cheap bargains to be had. However, a good quality lathe is an investment, so don't resent having to pay a bit more for it.

3·7   Working Height

A lathe which is to be worked continuously should be at a comfortable height for the operator, and operators do come in assorted sizes!

My principal lathe is set up to suit me, with the lathe centres at elbow height when I am standing on a duck board. I don't think an inch either way is critical, but a comfortable working position is important.

The height can be adjusted by either building a lathe stand of the appropriate height or by fitting blocks between the lathe feet and the top of the stand or bench (fig. 12).

12 Height adjustment for the lathe

This latter method of height adjustment will leave a nice big gap between the bed of the lathe and the bench top which will take tool and calliper racks, etc. (see chapter 1·6 for details of rack).

Rubber strips on the packing block faces help to dampen down vibration as well.

3·8 Tool Rests

Tool rests are a great talking point amongst turners.

My own preference is for a rest which has a parallel rear section, with a slight radius on the front face and a larger radius on the rear face, as shown in fig. 13.

13 A tool rest section

The front radius helps scrapers to traverse more easily on face plate work, whilst the rear radius has less tendency to sustain pitting on spindle turning, as it gives a more sympathetic surface to the tool than would a sharp edge.

It is also a good idea to have a selection of rests to suit different lengths of timber.

My eight or so Coronet rests vary in length from 36″ down to 2″, this latter being used for such work as thimbles and other short stuff.

And I subscribe to the school which calls it a tool rest or a hand rest, depending upon the type of work which is being done. It is most certainly NOT a tool guide.

3·9 Copying Devices

A couple of quick points just before we finish with lathes.

Whilst I have not by any means seen all the copying attachments on the market, I have yet to find an inexpensive one which is both safe in use and which leaves an acceptable finish on the work.

I think that a properly designed copy lathe can be operated by less skilled labour than a hand lathe, so if a large order comes along and extra help is needed to cope, then buy a good machine rather than a cheap one with an optional attachment. Of course, developments are being made all the time in this field, so shop around before you buy.

3·10 Grinding

The second point refers to grindstones.

I have seen photographs of turners grinding tools on unguarded wheels, allowing sparks and debris to get everywhere, including into the lathe bearings.

Use an independent and fully guarded grindstone where possible, thus keeping grit away from the lathe, but if you have to use a lathe mounted wheel, then at least for the sake of the lathe, have the wheel enclosed as much as possible.

I don't need to remind people to wear goggles when using a grinding wheel, do I?!

4 Turning Tools

4·1 Basic Choice

As this book is not aimed primarily at the novice turner, who is bemused by the number of lathes, tool sets and chucks on the market, but at the turner who has 'done a bit', I have not gone into any great detail on the wide range of available machinery, the reader probably already having made his choice.

Neither will I detail tools. The reader should have a basic knowledge of which tools do what work most efficiently and by now has probably got a selection of them in the workshop. Again, I would refer anyone who is unsure of basic requirements to the bibliography.

A criticism often levelled at professional turners is that they have too many tools. This opinion is usually voiced by people who turn, but do not earn a living from what they make.

I agree that a basic set of just three tools, a gouge, a parting tool and a skew chisel, can give hours of enjoyment. Incidentally, I recently heard the skew referred to as a 'stew', and I must admit to having met some people who have got into a stew trying to use it.

I also agree that the novice can be just as confused by a range of tools as he often is by the range of lathes, chucks, timbers and books available nowadays.

I have at least 40 tools in my collection, not many of them duplicated, and I have had need of them all at some time in the past.

A few I have made – or had made – for specific jobs, but most are standard.

One catalogue in front of me as I write, details no fewer than 60 different gouges and chisels, without considering scrapers.

The professional turner never knows what work will come through the door next and as new tools are bought for specific jobs, so the tool drawer gets heavier.

Most of the tools which I use were bought as they were needed rather than 'because they were there'. I do make the occasional impulse purchase, usually finding work for the tool once I have it, but the general rule is to only buy when necessity demands. And then, buy unhandled tools.

Naturally I make my own handles nowadays. That way the handle suits my own hand.

I don't like talking about tool 'balance' as the blade gets shorter with repeated grinding anyway, and so the balance will change. However, 'feel' is important.

I did say earlier that not many of my tools are duplicated, but certainly some are.

I teach turning, and if both students need the same tool then duplication is necessary. I also have a selection of ¼″ parting tools, one of which has a cutting edge which is honed as square and straight as possible. This tool I keep for producing the fit between base and lid on boxes.

4·2 Principal Choice for Spindlework

Basically, I have 3 square-ended roughing gouges, 1¼″, ¾″, and ½″ (see fig. 14a); 3 spindle gouges, ½″, ⅜″, and ¼″ (see fig. 14b); 3 skew chisels, 1″ long bevel for planing cuts, 1″ short bevel for turning the pummels on chair legs etc., and ½″ for short slender work (see fig. 14c). I also have a ¼″ parting tool (see fig. 14d). These are the spindle turning tools which I find I use most often.

14a Roughing gouges

14b Spindle gouges

14c Skew chisels

14d Parting tool

4·3 Choice for Bowls

For bowls, I use 3 gouges, ½" long bevel, ½" short bevel and ¼" (see fig. 15a). I also have a set of heavy duty scrapers which are used from time to time, but as most of my work is between centres, they don't come out of the drawer very often (see fig. 15b).

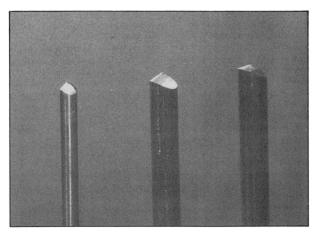

15a Bowl gouges

15b Bowl scrapers

4·4 Files, A Warning

Whilst on the subject of scrapers, one word of warning.

Many authoritative books speak of using old files as scrapers, giving details of how the teeth are ground away to expose the softer metal and the file is then shaped on the grinding wheel.

Not all of these books speak of the cracks

16 *Old files are not all they are cracked up to be*

which often occur during the file's manufacture (see fig. 16). No amount of annealing will rid the file of these cracks and the tool is likely to fracture at a crack if put under too much stress. The file in fig. 16 is, in fact, now used only to show other turners what to watch out for when deciding on the suitability of old tools.

I occasionally use old files, being as unwilling as most people to throw away good metal. But I never allow much overhang of the tool between the rest and the timber when working with such tools.

If in doubt, don't use files. A professionally made scraper is much cheaper than an eye, and what's more the only pain involved is to the pocket.

As I said earlier in this chapter, I do have a number of special tools – well, non-standard anyway, and these I will detail in chapter 8 on tool rôles and techniques in their use.

5 Sharpening

5·1 General

Speaking of using old tools, and earlier of impulse buying, I once paid a shopkeeper £1 and took away about 10 shallow carpenters' gouges which he had decided to clear out.

"Ideal for the lathe", I gloated.

Once I had put the bevel where it belonged on the outside of the tools rather than the inside, I set to work with the tools on the lathe.

I soon discovered that although the tools were made by one of the leading Sheffield tool houses, they were fine for carpenters, but wouldn't hold their edge on lathe work, due I suspect, to the greater work rate which the turner demands of his tools, coupled with the higher temperature at the point of cut.

I will probably anneal and then re-temper one of the tools some day, and if I get more wear out of it, then my £1 will not have been wasted. In the meantime, they make good pencil sharpeners, and the boxwood handles are probably worth a bit.

5·2 When to Sharpen

You usually know that a tool needs sharpening when it starts misbehaving.

That is an obvious thing to say, but I for one am frequently surprised at how much better a tool works when I put a new cutting edge on it.

Apart from the general feel, a good clue as to how the tool is working is to look at the shavings. This fact was brought home to me some years ago. I had asked an engineer friend to make me up a device rather like a large pencil sharpener, which was to point about 10,000 1″ diameter dowels.

Between us we produced the chuck, fitted it to the Major lathe and arranged a locating device to centralize the dowel prior to pointing it. I had just done the first half dozen trial pieces when a very experienced woodturner and machinist walked into the workshop.

I said, "Hey, Colin, come and look at what we've made".

The first thing he did was to pick up the shavings, glance at them and say "not much wrong with that Reg. Now, what are you doing?" Only then did he look at the chuck.

If the shavings are O.K. there's not going to be a lot amiss with the finish on the wood.

5·3 Grinding Angles

I am often asked at demonstrations what angle the tools should be ground to, and my answer is always that tool angles are important but not at all critical. And they often vary from one turner to another anyway.

I recently did an impromptu spell on another turner's lathe and with his tools. He favoured generally shorter bevels than I am happy with and it took me a couple of minutes to get the feel of them.

If, like me, you sometimes get lost when working out grinding angles, try recording the actual length of the tool bevel and its profile when it comes from the maker or when you find what suits best. (See fig. 17.) This way,

17 Parting tool bevel length

7/8″
(22mm)

you can measure and maintain working angles much easier when re-grinding. And usually when re-grinding, both the bevel and the memory of what it used to look like gets shorter with the passage of time. With a sketch to refer to, any significant changes can be seen easily.

I said, when speaking of bowl gouges, that I have two identical tools, but with different bevel lengths. (See fig. 15, chapter 4·3.)

The long bevel I use for most of my bowl work, but I find that I usually get a better cut on the inside base of a deep bowl with the shorter bevel.

Timber type and condition also affects the choice of tool and grinding angles. My only hard and fast rule here is that if one of the tools doesn't work then I try the other one. If neither work, the I re-sharpen them. If still no success then I go fishing.

5·4   Grinding Wheels

When grinding a tool on the wheel, I do now use the front of the wheel only, rather then its side.

Narrow grinding wheels are not made to take a side load.

If you don't understand what I mean, try putting side pressure on a rotating polishing mop and watch what happens to its shape. (See fig. 18.) The danger of a wheel shattering is to be avoided at all costs.

18   Grinding wheels don't flex as readily as polishing mops!

Using the front of the wheel then, means that the tools will be hollow ground, but for short bevels the tool handle is held high, whilst longer bevels can be obtained with the tool handle held lower. And should you require a flat bevel, it can still be obtained from the front of the wheel by lightly putting the cutting edge and bevel of the tool on the wheel and then lowering and advancing the handle, causing the bevel to ride up on the wheel.

I know that a lot of turners do not use the tool rest on the grinding wheel, but I generally do. I prefer to keep my finger under the rest and away from the debris produced by the grinding action of the wheel when possible. This means that the tool rest needs to be not only rigid but also square to the wheel, otherwise odd shapes can be found on parting tools after grinding – one point sometimes being shorter than the other. The front of the wheel should also be kept in good condition, of course, by using a devil stone or some other dressing device to true it and get rid of any glazing.

When shaping my turning tools on the grinding wheel I like to stand to one side and look at, as well as feel, the contact which the tool is making on the wheel. (See fig. 19.)

19   Grinding wheel and stance

This seemingly ungainly stance has two advantages to my mind. It allows the sense of sight to back up and confirm what I can feel of the tool on the wheel. It also allows for a greater arc of arm movement when grinding gouges and round nose scrapers. I was gratified recently to see David Ellsworth, one of the leading American turners, adopting the same stance, and for the same reasons.

5·5 Grinding Scrapers

When grinding scrapers I seem to be out on my own in that I do them upside down. That is, I actually offer the tool to the wheel with the cutting edge trailing. (See fig. 20.) My reason for this is that whilst most turners agree that a scraper usually needs a burr to work well, the burr produced by the wheel when the tool is ground cutting face up, must consist of a large proportion of wheel debris, which will crumble quickly.

20 *Grinding a scraper*

My method of grinding with the edge down allows the 'flowing' metal to form a burr which must surely contain less debris. And I still use a ticketer to restore a worn burr until the tool needs re-grinding. (See fig. 21.)

21 *Ticketing*

5·6 Grinding Jigs

I know of, but have not needed, tool grinding jigs for use with wheels. I may be wrong, for the umpteenth time, but I think that the jigs are a substitute for skills and not as versatile in use as a co-ordinated hand and eye. Also, many turners need a variety of angles on some tools, which the grinding jig can't achieve.

I have also seen drawings of honing jigs which looked as though they were designed by diamond polishers. I put them in the same category as the grinding jig.

5·7 Honing

Now to a great bone of contention. To hone or not to hone? I agree with Phil Reardon when he says in his Woodturners Pocket Book that the argument helps sell magazines. Keep buying them folks, we need the money!

I am a honer 95% of the time. Whilst I don't think that puts me on the endangered species list, I am almost certainly in the minority amongst my fellow professionals.

Honing doesn't take any longer to do than grinding. Nor is it messy. You see, I don't use oil every time.

The slip stone I use has been well soaked in a light oil and is kept wrapped in a cloth except when I am turning, when it lives on the bench but under the cloth to keep it from shavings and dust. The stone could even be used dry, but the presence of a light oil seems to provide a better cutting surface.

As regards cleaning the stone, I caused a minor tremor in the establishment a couple of years ago by announcing to the world that I discarded an old worn-out stone by throwing it into the workshop stove and then hurriedly closing the stove door, lest it should spit at me.

A few minutes later, I opened the door again and noticed that the stone had taken on the same cherry red glow as the coke it was sitting on.

Curiosity overcame me and I rescued the stone, allowed it to cool, and discovered that it had lost the accumulation of gunge and gloop which just about all the more orthodox cleaning methods had failed to dislodge.

And the phoenix-like stone worked once more, producing a cutting edge on my tools very quickly.

I now treat my carborundum slip stones in this way on a regular basis, but only slip stones, which don't come under any stress in use, of course. If you decide to experiment, then use a small piece of stone, keep the stove door closed, and allow the stone to heat up, and then, once removed with tongs, to cool down again at an even rate and on a sympathetic surface.

I prefer to use a slip stone to sharpen the tools, finding it easier to control than the ponderous bench stone. Holding the large tool still and moving the small stone makes sense to me. (See fig. 22.)

22 Honing

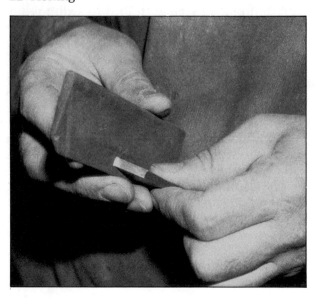

5·8   New Tools

When new chisels and scrapers arrive from the makers, they invariably have corners along the blade which are sharp and which need easing with an old slip stone to allow for easier traversing along the tool rest. Just a few light rubs is enough and it doesn't half make life easier! (See fig. 23.)

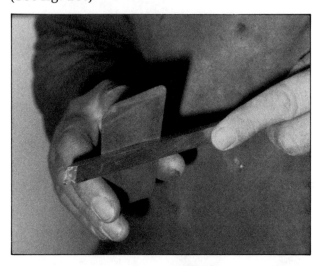

23 Radiusing the corners of a tool

I like to remove the sharp edges on the inside flute of gouges as well, not in this case for the comfort of the tool rest, but it saves having grooves cut into my hand on some operations.

5·9   Cleaning

I find that a piece of cloth tied to the tailstock end of the lathe is useful for the occasional wipe required by a newly-honed tool and also for any other similar wiping operations.

6 Timber: Selecting, Buying and Seasoning

6·1 General

Before we can actually start using our lathe and newly-ground and sharpened tools, we have to find something to work with.

As I have said elsewhere in this book, there are many pitfalls in the woodturner's world and the traps inherent in timber selection and buying have probably claimed more victims than our cat has fleas.

Very often the item to be made dictates the choice of timber and so the initial problems are eased, once basic knowledge of timber properties has been acquired.

I had a qualified school teacher working for me a few years ago. He wanted to get away from the classroom for a year or two and was 'drifting'.

In his spare time with me he made himself a new handle for his hammer. He made it from beech and is now back at school teaching art.

6·2 Properties

Different timbers have different properties, the cartwheel being a typical example of this fact.

The hub or stock was made from elm because its interlocking grain gave it the ability to hold together under stress despite all the holes which cartwheel hubs needed. Indeed, some examples which I have seen were more hole than hub.

The spokes were made from oak, principally, according to George Sturt's 'The Wheelwright's Shop', because of its acceptance of cleaving as opposed to sawing, but also certainly because it would stand up to the subsequent work load demanded of spokes.

The 'felloes', or 'fellies' – rim segments to we unenlightened ones – were made from ash, which is springy enough to take the shocks which uneven roads and tracks administered.

And had my schoolteacher friend known that ash would stand the shockwaves demanded of hammer handles, he would have saved himself a lot of time – and possibly a broken window as well.

6·3 Choice

On the subject of timber choice, I often find that the customer will provide material ready for the lathe.

When the customer is himself a woodworker, then this is usually to my advantage in that the prepared blanks should not only be suitable for the job but also, and this is almost as important, already paid for by him.

The problems occur however, when the timber selection wasn't done with either care or knowledge of the turner's requirements, or when I drop a clanger and have to match the wasted stuff at my own expense.

Below is a list of the more common faults to watch out for:

Short Grain: This is where the grain direction does not run for the full length of the timber. (See fig. 24, upper section.)

Knots: These are the bits of branches which reach right into the centre of the tree. O.K., obvious to most woodworkers, but I have met some who didn't know! Knots are not always enemies. Some actually make rather plain items much more attractive, breaking up the grain direction as they do. Knots in pine – if

24 *The wood at the top is short-grained idigbo. Below we see thunder shakes in Brazilian mahogany*

they have a black ring round them – are 'dead' knots, and are therefore likely to come adrift during turning, as they are loose. Even if the knot has no such ring it should still be treated with respect, for although it is not loose within the surrounding timber, it does have a grain direction which is different to that of the surrounding timber.

Splits or Shakes: These come, like blessings, in many forms.

End shakes are probably the most common, being caused by the fresh timber drying out at a quicker rate than the centre of the board, plank or trunk.

Ring shakes are so called because they follow the line of the growth ring all the way round its length.

Cup shakes are ring shakes that didn't quite make it all the way round.

Star shakes radiate from the centre of a tree towards its perimeter.

Radial shakes – run from the outside of the timber towards its centre and through the sapwood, but usually stop when they get to the heart wood.

Thunder shakes – these are faults in the grain which run haphazardly more or less at right angles to the direction of growth, but seem not to weaken the timber particularly (see fig. 24, lower section). This is in my limited experience of them, as I have yet to find one which was anything more than a meandering line, rather than an actual split.

There are also other natural faults to watch out for including, of course, worm holes and rot damage.

A few years ago, rotten or wormy timber would have been burned, but a number of turners far more adventurous than I, have produced saleable items which looked more like sieves or riddles than the bowls which they are described as.

In general I am in favour of using any piece of timber which can be worked safely and fashioned into something either useful or attractive.

Better to allow many generations of people to enjoy a 'spalted' bowl than for one or two people to benefit from a short-lived heat source. And anyway, the shavings from such a bowl can be cremated, giving satisfaction to devotees of both schools of thought.

There are also many sorts of unnatural faults to be wary of when buying timber, but not all of them are obvious until the saw starts its work.

Felling shakes are like thunder shakes but the fibres have actually been parted and remain so.

Drying shakes in the surface of the timber, showing often as short thin lines along its surfaces, are usually caused by bad kilning. Too fast – I suspect – or too slow, I don't know for sure. But I do know that I can't use the *!*!*! stuff, as the splits often go a long way into the wood, even sometimes, defying attempts to get sound 1″ square from poor 2″ square.

The final unnatural fault which I find all too often – and once in a lifetime is too often with these things – are foreign bodies.

The most expensive one which I have come across to date, cost me an 80 tooth, fine kerf, 18″ saw blade. And I never found what had been hidden in the German beech which I was ripping. My guess was that I had hit a bullet or a piece of shrapnel, but getting compensation from whoever had put it there in the first place, could have been problematical.

A colleague of mine once found a musket ball with the circular saw, the small flat which the blade left allowing the ball to 'sit on the mantel shelf a treat'.

Nails and other man-driven foreign bodies can be found in round timber and so the buyer should be very wary before venturing too far into the stuff with expensive machinery.

6·4 Ordering

Having found the right timber for the work, care should be taken in actually ordering it.

I once ordered 100 lengths of 4″ × 4″ iroko, each piece being some 30 inches long. These were for snooker table legs and were for a customer whom I had previously supplied with batches of a dozen or so.

I negotiated a better price with my timber supplier as I was now in 'The Big Time' on this job. I agreed that, as before on the smaller batches, I would take the off-cuts as well, paying for them, of course.

When the hundred prepared blanks finally arrived, the off-cuts pile was as big as the pile of turning blanks.

What I hadn't anticipated was that with the smaller batches, my timber merchant had selected the one or two most economical lengths of timber from the pieces on the top of his stock, so the off-cuts were minimal.

With a hundred blanks to find however, he had taken the top layers unselected and regardless of economy, thus giving me something close to a 50% wastage factor.

True, I sold the off-cuts, eventually, and made a profit on them. But I spent 18 months falling over the thundering things first. And I wanted my profit when the original work was completed, not months later.

I remember this episode as the great snooker table leg disaster. To help avoid such disasters now, I try to involve the timber merchant in my work, showing him what I am going to make from his timber. It gives him an interest in the project as well and, I like to think, gives him more inclination to find me the best timber for the work.

As I have already indicated, I often get the timber merchant to prepare the blanks for the lathe, when he can do it quicker and easier than I can. But you do have to know your merchant.

One chap I go to has a foreman who tries to help by giving generous measure.

This is good, except that the 29″ specified lengths sometimes come off the cross-cut saw at 30″. And when they are from 4″ square timber and there are a lot of them, and my accurate cross-cutting capacity is 2½″, it can be a bit trying. With friends like him, who needs enemies?

The present methods of converting logs at the mill, that is through and through, can produce some of the much sought-after quarter-sawn boards which are so ideal for bowls and flat work. (See fig. 25.) But watch out for the remnants of star shakes when you find them amongst the other boards – and they are almost certainly at the bottom of the pile. That is Sod's Law.

25 Quarter-sawn beech

6·5 Stocking

I do like to keep small stocks of some timbers, but I am a manufacturer, not a timber merchant and space, be it floor, wall or rafter, is too valuable to clutter up with a lot of wood that 'might come in handy one day'.

For general work I find that stocks of 1½″ and 2″ boards of beech and/or maple are the most useful.

The beech I prefer for teaching projects but the harder maple is better for its superior finish and long spectacular shavings.

It is, I find, a good idea to have a number of stock items in the craft range which can be made from the same-size boards, thus cutting down the range of sizes which I need to stock.

For instance, from 2″ beech I make rolling pins, rounders bats, and whipping tops, all good sellers in the right place. It is also a useful size for teaching exercises.

6·6 Drying

When converting timber for the lathe, particularly if the off-cuts are wet, interesting and not small enough to throw away, I date them and stack them to dry somewhere out of the weather but where the air can get at them.

About a year per one inch of thickness is a general rule of thumb for timber drying, but it depends on so many other factors as well; original moisture content, drying environment, type of timber. All these are contributing factors.

If the timber is particularly valuable then it can be weighed periodically, the weight and date recorded and when the weight reaches equilibrium, the wood is as dry as it can be in that environment.

6·7 Safety

One final word of caution on the subject of timber. Some timbers, particularly the imported ones, can cause skin and respiratory problems. For instance, I wear a respirator when working with both iroko and afrormosia.

Some of the exotics tend to 'get up my nose' as well.

The old axiom of 'it's vegetable matter and will therefore dissolve before it does any harm', just isn't good enough. Particularly nowadays, when a greater variety of species are available to the modern turner.

7 Marking – Setting

7·1 Work (at last)!

Now that we have lathes, tool selection and sharpening and also timber choice sorted out, we're ready to start making something with them all.

First of all we must consider marking out stock, setting callipers etc.

7·2 Finding Centre

I have a number of centre-finding jigs and aids which are detailed in chapter 17·2, but for general spindle-turning where the timber is 'full' (that is, oversize) I frequently guess where the centre of the work is and make a small diameter but deep hole at that point in each end of the stock. I've been guessing for some years now and I'm not often very far out.

If part of the work is to be left square, furniture legs or balusters for instance, or if it is only just big enough to produce the required diameter, then I use the ultra-accurate marking gauge (see fig. 26) or the not-quite-so-ultra pencil and fingers principle (see fig. 27).

7·3 Warped Timber

There are, however, occasions when finding the centre at each end of a square section of timber is not a great deal of use to the turner: I refer to those lengths of prepared timber which look as if they came from the banana tree.

I know that timber which is warped should not be turned. I also know that the text books say timber for turning should be straight, sound and knot-free.

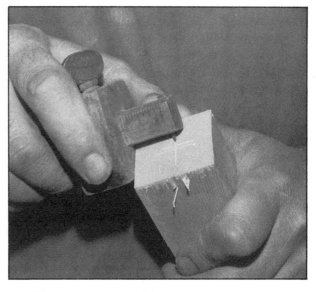

26 *Ultra-accurate marking gauge on pine*

27 *Usually acceptable pencil and fingers – also on pine*

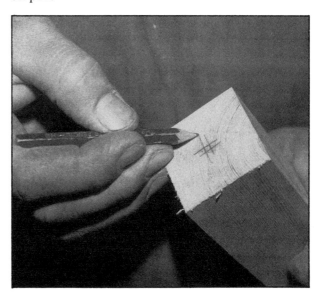

However, I am frequently reminded that ours is not an ideal world and warped timber is a fact of life.

What degree of eccentricity can be accepted depends upon the work being done, the lathe, the cost and general condition of said timber and the skills and/or desperation of the turner. Suffice to say that I have often been asked to pick out the best of a batch of prepared stair baluster blanks for instance, having been told ''There are a couple of dodgy ones so I've done some spares''.

When presented with these deviant departures from the straight and narrow, mark out the blank to show where the turned area is to be – it is usually more or less central, with a square section at each end – and then find and lightly mark actual centres at each end as described in chapter 7·4.

The bent blank is loaded on to the lathe, held lightly between centres and with the lathe running at a slow speed, a nick is made at each end, just inside the turned area, with a skew, long point down (see fig. 28).

28 'Nicked' – the timber is beech

With the lathe switched off, the nicks, or lack of them, show which way the timber should be moved at each end to centralize the area to be turned.

Moving the driving centre end is usually the easiest as the driving teeth, or dogs, can gain and hold a new position 'a bit further over than the last one', but the tailcentre, working in a vee, is not as easy to adjust.

Large adjustments can be achieved by making a new locating hole in the right direction, but small adjustments often need packing pieces down between the centre and the old hole, thus effectively moving the timber towards or away from the tool rest, whichever is appropriate. The lathe is then switched on again and the skew used as before, but not quite in the same place as last time, so that the new nicks are not confused with the old ones. These adjustments are made until the section to be turned is running true. And if you are faint-hearted, it doesn't pay to look at the eccentrically revolving ends. If you think this sounds like a dangerous practice, you're not wrong, but I make no apologies for detailing it, for as a professional turner I have had to do such things on more than one occasion over the years, and I suspect I am not alone.

7·4   Awls

Getting back to the hole-making devices, I have already said that I normally use a long slender awl, producing a hole which allows the centre to find its own way into the wood, with just a little guidance from the hole, when tightening up between centres. (More of this in chapter 9·1.) But timbers with alternating hard and soft rings can be a problem sometimes, especially when the centre coincides with a hard growth ring. I have found in these circumstances that a flat-nosed awl tends not to be diverted from its chosen course by the harder obstructions it comes up against.

Could that be, I wonder, why a lot of rugby players have flat noses?

7·5   Pin Sticks

The easiest way to explain my use of pin sticks in their many forms is to actually make a leg for a one-legged blanco stand (old army joke), which will involve some of them (see fig. 29).

The first operation is to mark out on the

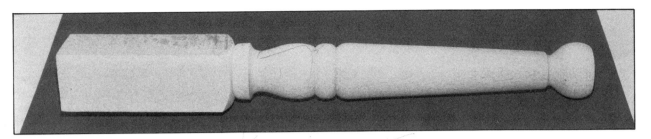

29a *Blanco stand leg*

29b *Blanco stand pin stick*

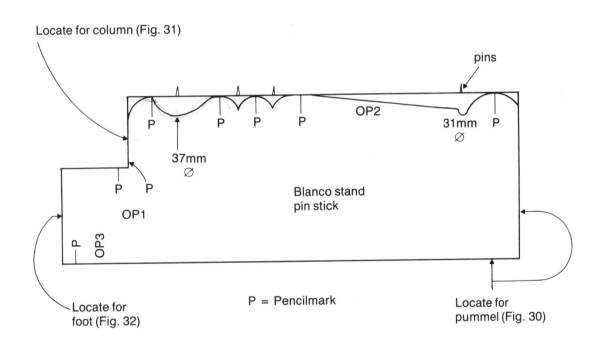

Locate for column (Fig. 31)

pins

OP2

P   P   P   P   31mm Ø   P

37mm Ø

P   P

OP1

Blanco stand
pin stick

P
OP3

P = Pencilmark

Locate for
foot (Fig. 32)

Locate for
pummel (Fig. 30)

stationary blank just where the pummel is to be and how long the corners are (see fig. 30).

The pummel mark is completed with a try square but the corner mark is left quite short (about ⅛″, 3mm) – this ensures that when both the marks are only just removed by the tool, then the sizes and lengths of shoulders on all the pieces within the batch will be consistent.

I generally use an HB pencil, which leaves quite a nice thin mark without giving me eye strain trying to see it. An alternative would be a carpenter's pencil, sharpened to a chisel point.

And don't forget, when marking out, that there is no need to mark all four faces. One is quite sufficient as it will show clearly when the timber is revolving.

Next I produce the pummel and the cylinder. Actually producing these pummels I deal with in chapter 8·12 on skews and their uses, so back to the marking.

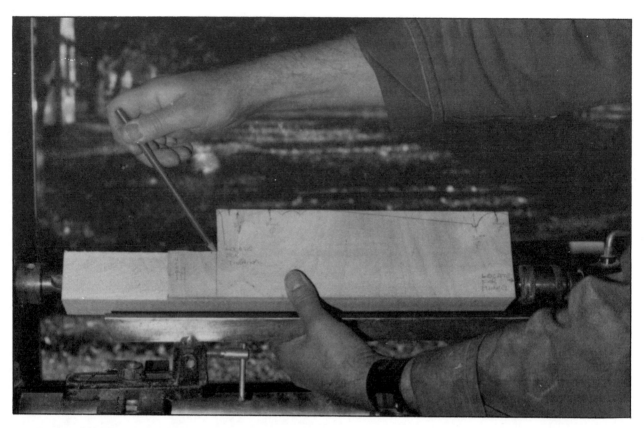

30 Pin Stick, stage 1. Marking the beech blank for pummel

31 Pin stick, stage 2. Marking rotating stock

The second stage in my use of the blanco stand pin stick shows a combination of both pins and pencil grooves (see fig. 31).

When the work has a pummel at one end only, then I often use the stick without switching the lathe off, merely adjusting the tool rest so as to bring it nearer to the revolving cylinder, but of course avoiding the rotating pummel. An element of danger? Yes, but I'm not writing specifically for the novice. I frequently adjust tool rests without stopping the lathe, but once again I've been doing it for a long time, I'm usually using a single round bed lathe, I'm in a hurry and there's an army out there waiting for its blanco stands.

Where there is more than one pummel then I do switch the lathe off to mark for stage two, and I suggest that you switch off for any marking where pummels are present. Don't do as I do – do as I say!

Should the work have no pummels at all, then cylinders can be marked quite safely with the lathe running, once the gap between the tool rest and timber has been adjusted, of course.

I tend to put both pins and pencil grooves together on the same stick quite often. The advantages of pins are that they leave more consistent marks and are quicker to use than pencils. The disadvantages are that they can't be used for marking tops of beads etc., without disturbing the surface of the work, and they also take some time to prepare, whereas a pencil groove can be quickly cut into the pin stick. Pencils can also be used to lightly mark the tops of beads and other high spots without destroying the surface of the work.

One final word on pencils, when used on revolving timber. Long pointed pencils soon get broken whereas a carpenter's pencil with its oblong lead can be sharpened to a chisel

32 *Pin stick, stage 3. Marking the foot*

edge, used on its side, made to locate in the pin stick groove, and will last a lot longer.

So the turning is produced, all but the foot. For this I use the lathe tailcentre to locate from and make a pencil mark where the turned area is to join the foot. (See fig. 32.)

As skills develop, or when the work does not demand such accuracy, then some of the marks can be omitted.

When making up pin sticks, it can sometimes be useful to have a range of standard sizes, giving distances of ½″, ¾″ etc., as I used to have.

Nowadays however, I usually make up a pin stick for each job which demands it.

The individual pins should all be the same length, should not protrude too far so that they don't bend in use, and can even be filed to achieve accurate sizing where needed (see fig. 33) such as when making time glass spindles, gallery spindles etc. For more information on pin sticks, see chapter 11·8.

33 *Pin stick for time-glass spindles*

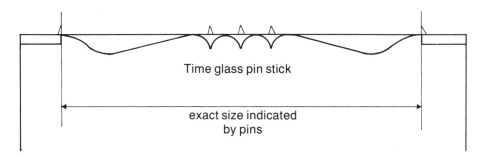

Time glass pin stick

exact size indicated
by pins

7·6 Ogee Pin Sticks

The ogee pummel is produced in a different way to that of the square-ended or rounded pummel and the method is detailed in chapter 8. However, the work is marked out as shown in fig. 34.

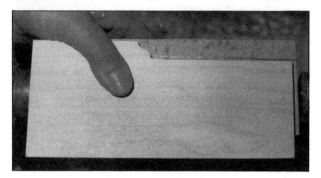

34 *Marking for ogee pummel on square of beech*

7·7 Sizing
(See also 8·2 and 12·2)

Just as important as marking out work for repetition turning, is the setting and use of callipers and other devices for accurate sizing.

As I tend to do my sizing operations with callipers in one hand and parting tool in the other (see fig. 35), I prefer to use spring callipers rather than the fixed type, although I do have both. I don't like the woodturner's 'sizing' tool for a number of reasons. First of all, if you need three or four callipering points on a

35 *Sizing the blanco stand*

job, and I regularly do work which requires more, then it is cheaper to buy extra callipers than extra parting tools and sizing tools. Secondly, the final part of a sizing cut has to be a scrape with the parting tool, as it is presented to the rotating timber at right angles. This takes the edge off the tool and also leaves a rougher finish on the surface of the wood.

The third reason for my dislike of the sizing tool, is that the whole assembly has to take up more bench space than a pair of callipers.

I must admit however, that the sizing tool is consistent and so if confidence or experience are lacking, then it has a place on the bench.

I do, however, think that the copying fingers supplied by one company are a good idea, although I don't use them myself, having invested in ten or so sets of callipers a few years before the fingers were readily available.

As can be seen in fig. 36, I have two adjusting nuts on the callipers, one locking against the other, so that they have less chance of undoing in use thus causing the callipers to open and diameters to increase over a batch of work. It is both embarrassing and expensive to have to rectify work which has been returned by a feather-spitting customer. I speak from experience.

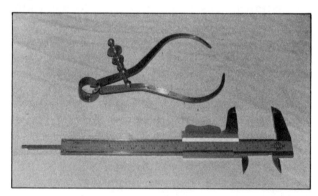

36 *Spring and Vernier callipers*

I also put a pencil mark on the top nut when the callipers are set. A quick glance then tells me that if the mark has moved away from its 6 o'clock position, the callipers need resetting. That's what is known as belt and braces.

Another modification which should be carried out to callipers when using them as I do, is to 'soften' or put a radius on the end of each leg, where it bears against the rotating wood.

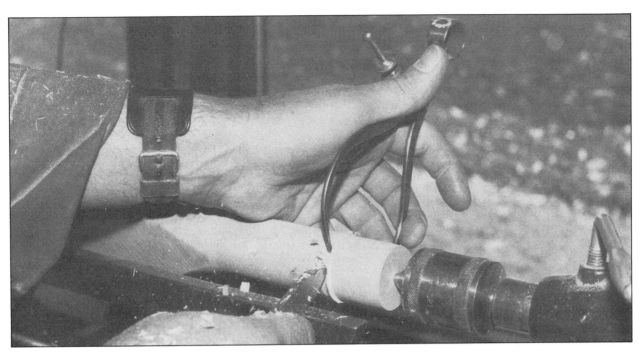

37 *Cushioning the whip in a length of maple*

38 *Roughing with a bowl gouge and using maple*

This helps to guard against the callipers catching in open-grained timber. And when sizing with parting tools and callipers, make certain that the unseen lower leg of the callipers is working in, rather than alongside the parting tool groove.

There are times when the parting tool and callipers combination won't work for sizing cuts. I usually find this problem an irritation on slender or 'whippy' work.

A slight amount of whip can often be cushioned by the heel of the calliper hand acting as a steady (see fig. 37), but excessive whip can defy most means of steadying the work when sizing.

A method I have evolved, and which I find useful under these circumstances, is to size as I go.

Starting at whichever end of the work is the most convenient, I use a bowl gouge on its side; supporting the revolving stock and holding the cutting end of the gouge firmly down on to the tool rest with one hand, then taking small cuts into the wood rather than along it. Figure 38 shows more clearly what I mean.

The sizing cut when I get to it is done a little at a time, the callipers being tried after each cut rather than during it, as one hand is always

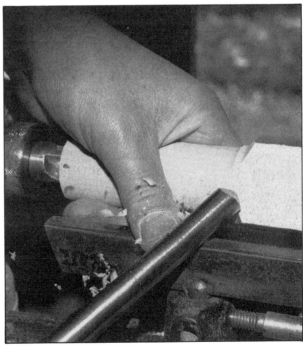

supporting the revolving stock whilst it is being either cut or sized. (See fig. 39.)

The detail here is also produced as I go, one hand supporting both the revolving timber and whichever tool is being used at the time.

Slow but sure is the order of the day on such

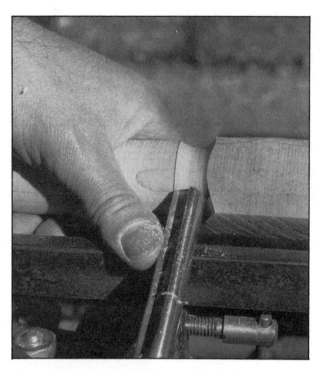

39 *Preparation for sizing*

work. And I don't mind using abrasive paper afterwards either.

One final point about setting. I do have an expensive Vernier calliper, graduated in both imperial and metric, of the type which an engineer would use (see fig. 36).

I do not use this tool on rotating stock, for the same reason that engineering apprentices are discouraged from using micrometers as 'G' clamps.

8 Tool Rôles and Techniques

8·1 How and Why

"Whenever I get a job to do which I have not tackled before, I usually think about it for a while, then have a go.

If it does not work out as I expect, I then search through the books I have on woodturning for clues as to how the job was done in the past or how it is done by other turners.

I frequently find that what seems to be a problem at the time can be overcome by a slight variation of what has been a basic skill or knack, itself learned at great cost in terms of lost production time in the past, then subsequently applied without thought once it had become part of the repertoire."

I wrote that four years ago in one of my 'Diary of a Woodturner' articles in *Woodworking Crafts*, the forerunner of *Woodworking International*, and it is just as true today. I am always learning and trust that I will carry on doing so for many years to come.

Some of the suggestions in this chapter I have discovered in books. Some have been born of necessity and then subsequently seen in books which were new to me and some are, I think, in print for the first time.

8·2 Hand Support
(See also 7·7 and 12·2)

There are times when it is necessary to support the revolving stock with one hand whilst using a tool with the other.

When I first started turning I read that this was common practice amongst the older craftsmen, but I told myself there was no way I would either touch the revolving wood or use a tool one-handed.

I now find myself doing both of these things quite often, sometimes even without the job demanding it, but always of course, with due consideration for safety.

I am naturally right-handed, but there are times when I have to work with the left hand only, the right hand may, for instance, be supporting a wooden egg which is about to leave its mother, the lathe (see fig. 40), or coaxing a

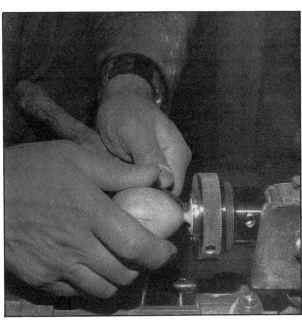

40 *Working one-handed on an idigbo egg*

spindle away from its preferred path over the top of the turning tool when a bead is needed to the right of a long pummel (see fig. 41).

To sum up then, I have learned to be ambidextrous in some work and it does make life easier once the learning curve is over. I am reminded of the chap who said "I'd give my right arm to be ambidextrous".

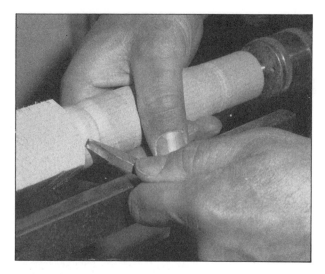

41 Working one-handed, and back on to the maple

This 'either hand' principle can be applied in many of the situations in this chapter.

8·3   Roughing Gouge

The roughing gouge (see fig. 14, chapter 4·2) is a tool which can do a lot more work than just making the square stock round. (I sometimes find myself referring to this operation as 'knocking the corners off' but 'roughing out' sounds better.)

When I am working in public I usually employ the 'a bite at a time' method, with my front hand under the tool (see fig. 42).

42 A bite at a time into short-grained beech

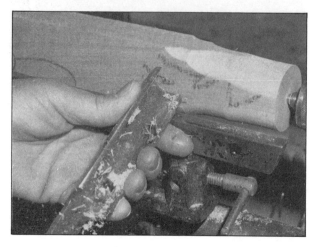

Although this is usually done right-handed, it can sometimes be advantageous to change hands if, for instance, I am working in a confined space or next to a stall full of woolly jumpers.

The advantage of this is that it stops the public from getting covered in shavings, most of them going behind me, rather than into the crowd. The last thing I need is someone trying to retrieve a sharp bit from inside a shirt, rather than wanting to buy my handiwork. And they don't like it when I accuse them of stealing my wood!

When I am on my own, I use the overhand method (see fig. 43). It is much quicker and I

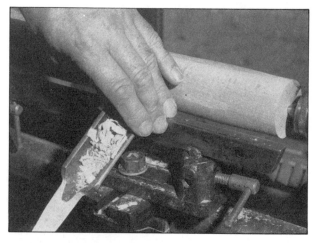

43 Overhand roughing

43a The business end of a roughing gouge

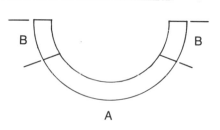

can work along in either direction, merely altering the tool angle slightly at the end of each pass, in order to cut on the return pass as well. I use my thumb and whichever finger will reach, to keep the tool rest clear of debris in front of the traversing tool.

The palm of the deflecting hand also shoots the chippings forward and away from me.

When using this hand over the top method, I find that once the actual corners of the work are removed and the exposed turned surfaces become larger, then the shavings are longer and less likely to fly over a large area.

And so, after a few cuts overhand, I transfer to the underhand grip and allow the now longer shavings a free flight to the floor behind me.

Some of the books on turning which I have read, advise the turner to rotate the tool as much as possible during this actual roughing cut, thereby giving the cutting edge of the tool more even wear. This makes good sense, but I have modified the principle slightly in that I only rotate the tool sufficiently to use half of its cutting edge – the middle half – whilst roughing. (See section A on fig. 43a.)

Sections B or the 'wings' of the tool, I keep for finishing cuts, using the flat sections rather like a planing cut with a skew chisel (see fig. 44). I find that I can get an acceptable finish on most timbers this way. Indeed, on short-grained timber, it seems to leave a better finish than the skew, which tends to lift the fibres and tear them.

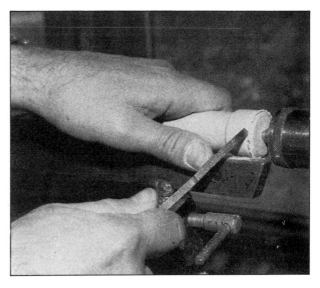

45 *Beading on a beech rounders bat with a parting tool*

And the final finishing cut runs from just inside the knob end of the handle right along, both downhill and uphill, to the end of the blade.

8·4 Deflecting with Thumb

When using some gouges I find myself occasionally deflecting shavings with the thumb and holding/guiding the tool just with the fingers (see fig. 46). Don't just stand there and accept a nostril full of shavings. Be inventive.

46 *Be inventive!*

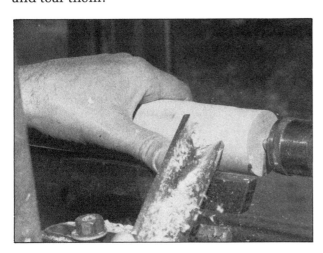

44 *Cutting with the wing*

The roughing gouge can also be used successfully on slightly uphill cuts, which are against the grain on most work (not all, see chapter 19·4).

To illustrate this, I often make rounders bats in beech, using just the roughing gouge for everything but the three radii. For these I use my good old parting tool (see fig. 45).

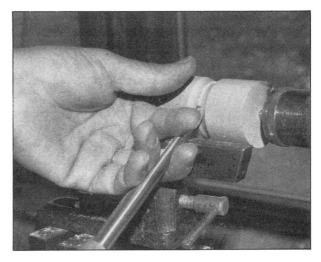

8·5   Coves

When I need to produce coves, internal radii or, as some of my unenlightened customers call them, 'bits that go in', until a few years ago I would have used the 'point of entry' method with a long-nosed spindle gouge, thereby suffering the occasional thread which runs along the surface of the wood and is familiar to most of us (see fig. 47).

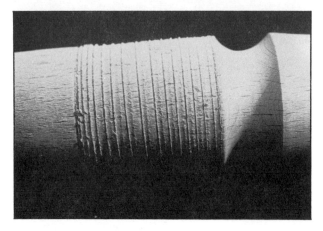

47 'Groovy' beech

I also found that this method produced a highly-polished area just inside the cove on some timbers, where the bevel is pushed into the newly exposed surface of the wood.

To overcome this burnishing problem, I started the cut with the wing of the gouge rather than the point. I had discovered that by presenting the tool not with its flute at 90° to the tool rest, but rather at about 75°, depending upon the shape of the tool nose, I didn't get the burnish.

This resulted in a better entry hole but also in more threads along the surface as the bevel couldn't get in behind the cutting edge to guide it.

Then a very nice Canadian turner, who was visiting this country and who was kind enough to call in and see me, showed me the grip shown in fig. 48.

The tool can't skate away as it is supported by either the fingers or the thumb, depending on the direction of the cut, the supporting hand being 'clamped' to the tool rest by its index finger.

Once the cut has started, then the bevel can

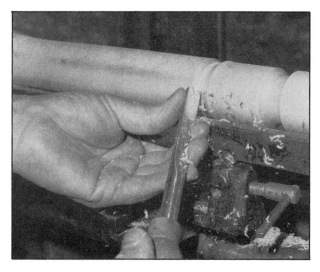

48 Underhand clamp

reach the cove and do its job, which is to guide the cutting edge.

I haven't seen or heard mention in any other work of this method – but I haven't read all the books by any means. Anyway, thank you Bert Thompson.

8·6   Ogee Pummel Cut

Another cut with a gouge which two very authoritative books talk about but don't show in any detail, is the ogee pummel cut.

Whenever I am required to produce these in any quantity, I usually make up a marking stick (see fig. 34, chapter 7·6). The pummel marking detail can of course, be incorporated into the normal pin stick detailed in chapter 7·5 should the job require such a pattern.

I use a long-nosed spindle gouge for the actual cuts, watching the 'up' side of the work to see and remove the waste timber where it was marked. Figs. 49 and 50 show the tool process in more detail. This cut is not easy to master. Witness the cry of the turner when it goes wrong. "Oh! gee!" he says with feeling. Well, it's Oh! something like that anyway!

8·7   Beads

Cutting beads can be fun. As I have said elsewhere, but not in this book, the first time I read

49 Halfway down the cut in 3" square beech

50 Almost there . . .

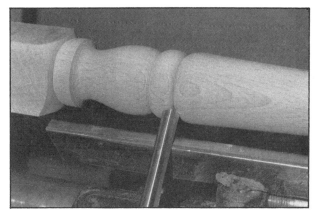

51 Problems with a spindle gouge and back on to the beech

that a parting tool can be used for this operation, I laughed my socks off.

Then I tried it and apologised to the chap who wrote the book.

Since I started teaching, I show how to cut beads, using skew, parting tool and gouge.

I also explain that whilst I usually use a parting tool for this work, I sometimes have to use whichever of the other tools performs best under the prevailing circumstances.

For instance, a spindle gouge will cut large diameter beads with more control than a parting tool but can't get into tight corners without one of its edges scraping the opposite wall (see fig. 51).

A parting tool can get into the tighter corners but is not as efficient on large diameters, or where the tool rest can't get close to the work, causing the parting tool to work with a lot of overhang.

The long-bevelled skew chisel can get into tighter corners than either of the others and can also reach further over the tool rest without loss of control. It is horses for courses. Whatever suits you is what you use for preference, but don't be frightened to experiment.

I recently had to produce some 20mm long gallery spindles, each one having two beads on it, the smallest of which was 1.5mm wide.

My favoured parting tool made a right dog's dinner of the first bead, but a small spindle gouge created no problems whatever.

As I have said, my students are shown three methods of beading, each one usually being practised before the next one is introduced.

One final hint which I can boast of discovering – although I suspect I am its umpteenth discoverer – is one which is useful when producing what could be described as sunken beads (see fig. 52).

The problem with such a job is that the shavings have nowhere to go on the initial cut, as opposed to the raised bead, where they fall away from the work freely.

I have borrowed the Frank Pain method of starting a pummel cut with a skew and applied

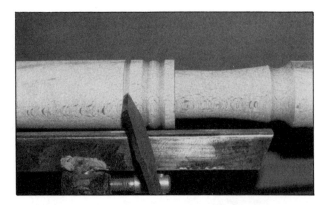

52 *'Sunken bead' and initial cut into beech*

it to a parting tool which produces the angled entry cut (see fig. 52).

The presentation of the tool to the wood is most important, otherwise the bead may be undercut or the grain lifted out by the corner of the top bevel (see fig. 53).

Having produced a vee on each side, the bead is now cut in the normal way, the resultant shavings having somewhere to go rather than hanging about the working surface and obscuring the view.

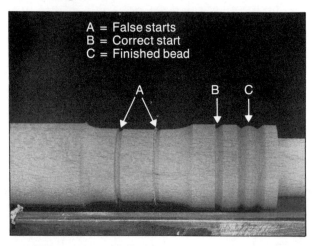

A = False starts
B = Correct start
C = Finished bead

53 *Two 'noes' and a 'yes'*

I have not mentioned the beading tool here, which is probably a terrible omission. But I haven't got one and so I can't comment on its use. It is, generally speaking, a broader and sometimes not so deep, parting tool – one catalogue describing it as a ⅜" (9mm) square section tool, with a chisel point and two equal bevels, each one about ½" in length.

8·8   Parting Tool

The parting tool (see fig. 14, chapter 4·2), really a chisel, is more versatile than its name suggests. Read on:

An engineering lathe turner uses the tool to part-off finished work. The woodturner does the same operation with the same tool, although it sometimes has modifications. More of this in a moment.

When using the tool on deep cuts, whether parting off or sizing, I often hear other turners give the same advice as that given by the choreographer to the chorus line girl. ''Waggle it about'' they both say.

The trouble with waggling the parting tool about is that whilst this will certainly achieve a wider cut than the tool could give if fed straight into the wood – thus avoiding the danger of the tool binding – it will not only leave rough surfaces on each of the walls, but also wear out the tool points, which are so important on beading operations.

Better, and I think no slower, to make the wider groove by using the tool in stages, each cut slightly overlapping and proceeding a little further than its predecessor (see fig. 54).

With practice, this can be done very quickly

54 *'Don't waggle it about'* – *beech once more*

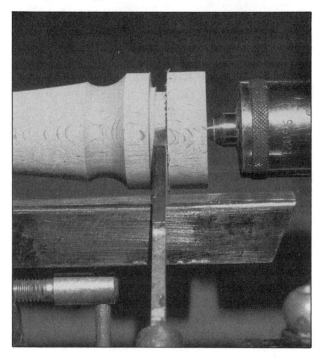

one-handed, the other hand either supporting the timber or holding the callipers, depending upon the purpose and position of the cut.

I am also concerned by the often offered advice to 'raise the parting tool handle' when doing sizing or parting cuts.

Surely the tool must also be advanced over the tool rest to maintain bevel contact with the newly-exposed face, otherwise the cut becomes a scrape at cost to both the tool edge and the face it is producing. (See fig. 131, chapter 16·5.)

8·9 Diamond Parting Tool

A word on diamond shaped parting tools. (See fig 55.)

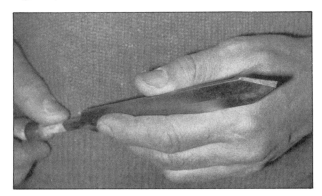

55 *Diamond-shaped parting tool*

I find them no better in everyday use than what has now become the normal-shaped parting tool, that is one which was originally designed by John Sainsbury, and has a slight but regular taper running along its length, from cutting edge back to, and including, the tang.

Indeed, on some operations the narrow top and bottom of the diamond tool can be a hindrance by causing the tool to either wobble on the rest or by gathering debris in the wedge-shaped gap between the tool and wall sides.

However, I do find the tool ideal when making slight undercuts on rings etc., as its relieved top edge often gives clearance to the outer wall (see fig. 56), whereas the standard parting tool would rub, at least destroying the corner of the work if not actually causing the tool to move laterally.

56 *Clearance on undercuts in captive ring from beech*

8·10 Skew-ended Parting Tool

I have a ⅛″ parting tool with a skew end giving a long and a short point. (See fig. 57.) I find this tool most useful for putting the slight dovetail on the spigot which is needed for some chucks. That was not, however, its original purpose.

When parting work off completely, a small 'nib' is usually left on one or both of the faces

57 *Skew ended parting tool*

58 *Nib left by standard parting tool. Yew blank is held in a Craft Supplies Ltd Spigot Chuck*

59 *Skew ended two flute parting tool*

of the wood. (See fig. 58.) And which face is to boast this nib is something of a lottery, but it is usually to be found on what should be the good face. Sod's Law strikes again.

My skew-ended parting tool allows me to decide which face is to have the nib, as it will be on the face which the short point is producing. Clever, ain't it?!

8·11   Two Flute Parting Tool
(See also 15·3)

The best tool for parting off however, is the two flute tool, used points down. And I have even put a skew on that! (See fig. 59.) It can be seen that the long point will precede the short point on any right angle parting cut, thus again giving control over which face is to be free of protuberances.

The tool can't however, be used upside down, so two tools would be needed should the choice of good face vary from job to job.

One thing against this type of tool is that the sharp edges wear holes in the tool rest in use, as well as putting at risk what will be the future points of the tool when it is older and shorter.

My solution to this problem was to fit a short length of plastic binding to the edge of the tool, cushioning its contact with the rest.

It was gratifying to me when a student of mine bought one of these tools some months after my idea was published, and the new tool came complete with plastic binding. Years ago tool manufacturers made what they wanted to, but now that turning is more popular, the makers are spending much more time listening to, and watching out for, ideas from turners. And that is the way it should be. Well done, everybody!

8·12   Skew Chisels

I was doing a demonstration a few years ago and was being asked technical questions by one of the customers – a lady.

We discussed the roughing gouge, we looked at the spindle gouge and we contemplated the parting tool.

During these minutes she told me that she was interested in turning, but had not actually tried it. All her information had come from the written word.

When I took up the 1″ skew, she took a pace backwards. When we exchanged amused smiles at her reaction, she said "Its reputation has preceded it".

The lady in question subsequently became my first female pupil, bought her own lathe and is now enjoying her turning, including working with the skew.

Whilst it is true to say that the skew is the tool most likely to misbehave in the hands of a novice, the effort needed to understand the tool will be well rewarded.

I am going to deal with the subject of dig-ins later on in this chapter and certainly the skew seems to take the lion's share of these 'cuts in the wrong direction'.

I have two 1″ skew chisels (see fig. 14c, chapter 4·2), the short bevelled tool I use for pummels and the longer bevelled one I use for planing cuts.

The short bevel will provide much more support for the cutting edge than the longer bevel, although the edge is not as sharp.

Making pummels tends to knock an edge about a great deal and the more robust short bevel is better able to withstand this battering.

I have seen two methods of making pummels with a skew. Until recently I used Frank Pain's way, which is to cut a vee section out of the rotating corners in one pass with the long point (see fig. 60). Even on large section timber it is possible to use this method without risking 'wrong directionitis', by starting away from the line and taking a series of single cuts, making each cut deeper than the last, until the required depth and position is reached. (See fig. 61.)

The right-angle corner which is left in the rotating wood after the cut can be softened or rounded if required, again using the skew but this time more upright (see fig. 62). For this second cut, the part of the bevel just behind the point must be rubbing on the newly exposed surface, otherwise we are likely to suffer another attack of 'wrong directionitis'.

Should the work being done require a square edge, then the second stage, 'softening', is omitted.

Frank Pain's 'The Practical Woodturner' should be consulted for more information on this particular method of turning. It is not my place to go into too much detail regarding basic tool techniques as this book would be too long, too heavy and too expensive if I added my name to the long list of turners who have explored and explained the basics.

I said that I know of two methods of producing pummels with the skew.

60 Pain's pummel production. 'Once more into the beech, dear friend!'

61 Series of starting cuts in beech

62 'Softening'

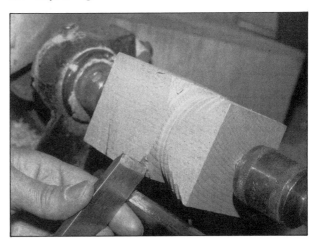

63 Slow but safe

The second one, which I am starting to use for preference, is to make a small 'vee' cut from each side of the pencil line, alternating and deepening with each cut until the depth and position of the 'vee' is achieved (see fig. 63). The tool is used in the nearly upright position as in the second stage of Frank Pain's method.

This method seems to take a little longer, although there is probably less likelihood of a dig-in.

The second of my 1″ skews is, as I have said, used for planing cuts, particularly after a pummel has been produced and its base needs cleaning up.

As I have already said, I tend to do a lot of planing cuts with the wing of a roughing gouge (chapter 8·3) but I do also use the long bevel skew for this work.

A lot of my students have trouble with the planing cut, principally because they don't have the tool under proper control.

Once I have explained that ideally the turner needs three points of contact with the tool – two hands and one side – then things seem to go a bit easier, as the tool has less tendency to wobble about.

Next come the feet. They must take a stance wide enough to allow cuts to proceed in as long a traverse of the work as possible, without the stop-start marks which indicate a change of foot position.

To avoid dig-ins, see chapter 8·13.

One more use of the skew which I find useful is when doing a sizing operation with parting tool and callipers where, for whatever reason, one side of the groove wall is to be left on the finished work.

The parting tool produces a rather rough wall, due to the cutting action of the tool.

If the sizing cut is made about $\frac{1}{16}$″ away from the finishing line, the rough surface can be removed by using the skew to slice up to the line, leaving a nice clean face (see fig. 64).

One final thought on the skew. Frank Pain shows it being used on a concave cut, and I do this myself from time to time, when conditions dictate.

64 Slicing cut with a skew

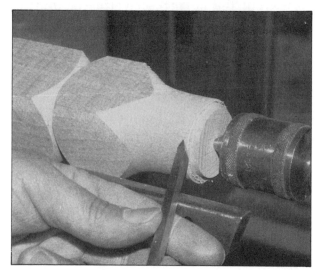

65 Coves with a skew

I have heard of a turner who used nothing but a skew on his pattern-making work, doing all operations with it.

It is certainly a tool which is more versatile than its shape would suggest. Try using it for shallow coves (see fig. 65).

8·13   Dig-ins

Why does a tool dig-in? Almost invariably because it is not being supported correctly.

Tool support comes from three areas. The turner, the tool rest and the work.

Turning tools usually have long handles, not to make them easier to find amongst the shavings but to allow the turner more control in producing those shavings.

The turner should have three points of contact with the tool, as I said in the last section. Two hands grip the tool and the body steadies it.

There are times when the tool has to lose one or even two of these supports, but these occasions should be kept to a minimum.

For instance, if I am parting-off an egg from the chuck with a skew, I am guiding the tool with the left hand and feeding the tool over the rest by pushing the back of the handle with my body (see fig. 40, chapter 8·2).

And when I am sizing with a parting tool, I have to work one-handed, although my grip on the tool has changed so that the hand, and sometimes even the arm as well, is holding and supporting the tool. (See fig. 66.)

This will help to overcome the tool's tendency to 'snatch'.

Another reason why tools sometimes go off and do their own excavation work is that they are not being supported correctly by the tool rest.

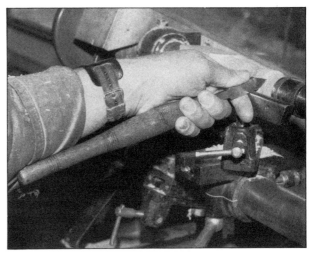

66 Maximum support from one hand

The general rule here is that the tool should be supported on the rest in a direct line with the point of the cut. Consider a gouge cutting a ball. Fig. 67 shows the operation as it should not be done from the turner's point of view. The upright tool is cutting with its wing and yet it is supported at its base, giving the tool a natural tendency to twist over to the left.

Fig. 68 shows what the turner should see whilst the cut is being completed.

The relevance of tool contact on the rest and corresponding cutting edge and bevel on the work is one which many people do not appreciate. This can be shown by using the example of the skew chisel on a planing cut.

I often ask other turners who are watching me at demonstrations, what would happen to the tool if I made the cut too close to the long point.

"It would dig-in", is the usual answer.

But when I ask them why, not many can answer.

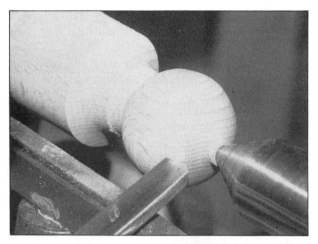

67 *Not like this – not even with beech!*

69 *Too close to the long point for comfort*

68 *. . . like this . . .*

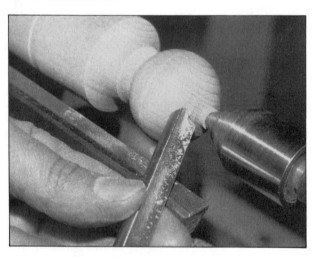

Once you know why things go wrong, and not just accept that they do, then you have a greater understanding of what mischief the tool and the wood are getting up to.

The skew will dig-in because it is being supported by the rest on one corner of the blade and its edge is being asked to work some way away from this support. (See fig. 69.)

The short point is almost always in line with the place of contact on the tool rest whilst the vagrant-like long point is further away, and without visible means of support.

If the planing cut is made at the **S**hort point it is **S**afe, but if the cut gets too close to the **L**ong point, then you are **L**iving dangerously.

How close to the long point the cut can be made, depends upon many things, not least of which is the skill of the turner. The general

rule however, is that the cut should be made no more than half way along the cutting edge from the short point.

Yet another reason for tools to misbehave is that the bevel of the tool has lost its contact with the work. I am not of course speaking of scrapers here, but gouges and chisels.

The bevel should rub the surface which the cutting edge has just exposed, for two reasons, which I will come to in a moment. When I say bevel, I don't mean the whole bevel of course, but whichever part, or parts, can rub safely.

If, for instance, a bead is being cut with a gouge, skew or parting tool, then a small area just behind the cutting edge of the tool should be in contact with the work.

Cutting a cove on the other hand is likely to produce two points of contact. One just behind the cutting edge of the tool and the other one at the opposite end of the bevel, its actual position depending upon the shape of the gouge and the depth of the cove.

Now then, to the two reasons for this contact. They are, in no particular order, for the protection of the cutting edge, and control of the direction the cut is to take.

First, protection . . .

If a gouge or chisel is offered up to revolving timber 'square on' (see fig. 70), then the edge is scraping and will soon be worn away. Also the surface of most timbers do not enjoy this experience either. Try scraping a new point on to a pencil to see what I mean. (See fig. 71.)

Much better to get the cut as in fig. 72, where

70 *Not this way*

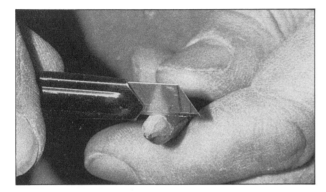

71 *. . . and not this way . . .*

72 *. . . but this way!*
73 *. . . or this way*

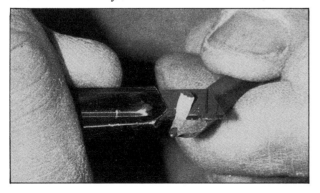

a small area of bevel is working on the newly-exposed surface, stopping the cutting edge from being too greedy and thereby self-destructing. Go back to the pencil again and you will see what I mean. (See fig. 73.)

A bonus of this bevel-rubbing action is that the new surface is also being burnished whilst the cut is in progress.

Now to the other reason for bevel contact. That is directional control. The cutting edge of a tool is a greedy little beggar. It will bite off more than it can chew, given half a chance.

To prove this, if you haven't already found out the hard way, try turning a coconut shy ball with a gouge, between centres.

When working, for instance, left to right and from the full diameter to the tailcentre, get a cut going and then lift the bevel away from the work by moving the right hand round in its arc a bit too soon.

You did want a spiral on the ball, didn't you? Yes, of course you did, it helps to give the ball some spin through the air!

When my students are doing this kind of work I say to them ''The bevel controls the direction and you control the bevel''.

Having got a cut going with a gouge or a chisel, think not of the cutting edge of the tool, but of the small invisible area of bevel just behind the edge. Now make that unseen area move in the direction needed to achieve the desired shape. But remember not to ask the tool to take a cut which would be too heavy. It's the combination of cutting edge and bevel which give the control during such a cut.

Finally, back to the skew chisel and planing cut for a moment.

We all know that a skew starts in from the end of a cylinder on this cut, so as to give the cutting edge some support by making contact with the bevel first.

In fact, some of us also know that a controlled cut can be started right on the edge of the cylinder, meaning that the cutting edge makes contact first, but without the expected dig-in. This is achieved by holding the tool more firmly and moving it along the work as soon as the cut has started, so as to bring the bevel into contact with the new surface as soon as possible.

Whilst this is a time saver, it can lead to confusion amongst innocent watchers, who are

likely to go away and practise the cut, with
dire results. I do this cut from time to time, but
only in isolation or accompanied by an explanation. I never do it without comment, should
I have an audience.

8·14   Tool Rest Position

I tend to work with the tool rest lower than
most turners when spindle turning. The
reason for this is that if the rest is too high then
the shavings tend to fly up and seem to arrive
at, or near, the neck line.

It's when they subsequently find their way
down inside my shirt to the nether regions that
the problems start. Cowboys are not the only
people who walk tall!

If the rest is lower, the shavings' trajectory is
somewhat flatter and my wife doesn't have to
vacuum the bedroom carpet so often.

Unless I am doing work with a chuck or
occasional spindle work with a scraper, I
usually leave the rest at the same height
throughout, compensating for this time saving lack of adjustment by working further up
on the wood with some cuts, but maintaining
contact with the tool rest of course.

8·15   New Methods

It is always a good idea to look at alternative
methods of doing some jobs, as I have already
said when talking about beading with a parting tool. Personal preference usually determines what tool is used for which cut.

For instance, I once had a problem with cutting vee grooves in fishing rod butts, or
handles (see fig. 74). As each butt had something like ten grooves and I did the butts in
batches of 100 or so, I investigated ways of
overcoming the irregularity problems which
came from my use of skew or parting tool.

The poor old vee-nosed scraper didn't help
much either, needing too much attention from
the grindstone, too often, and even then not
leaving a particularly good surface on the
work.

Reference to Frank Pain's 'The Practical
Woodturner' reminded me of the bruzze (see
fig. 75). The tool was machined for me from

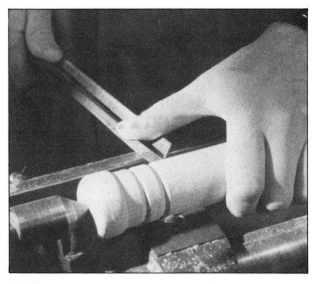

74 Bruzze in use

75 Bruzze

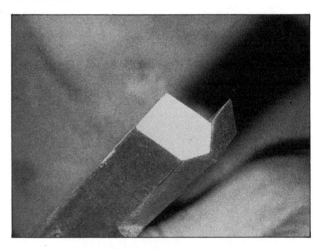

¾" square section steel of some sort – it was a
piece which had been lying around for some
time – fitted with a handle and then ground
back to give a point and two long 'wings', the
bevels of which were hollow ground.

I found the tool behaved quite well in use,
but tended to skate along the tool rest if one of
the wings got more than its fair share of work.

A modification to the base of the tool resolved this problem in that I replaced the
single point of contact on the tool rest with a
flat section, produced on the grindstone. This
gave better contact with and therefore more
control from, the tool rest.

I suspect that Frank Pain's bruzze was used
principally with a wooden tool rest, having

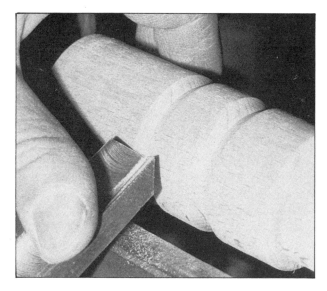

76 Bruzze in use (from a different angle)

notches either cut or worn into its top edge which the tool would sit in, and so be held steady in use.

The advantages of the bruzze were that I was cutting with a shearing action, not scraping, thereby achieving a more acceptable finish on the timber. Also I was working both sides of the groove from one position on the tool rest, which resulted in greater consistency of angles throughout the whole batch of rod butts. Fig. 76 shows the tool in use from a different angle.

I made something like 2,500 of those butts and had less than ten rejects from the customer. So pleased was he with this record that he gave me one of the finished rods, a 50lb. class boat rod, for my own use.

But I have yet to catch anything with it.

8·16 Dovetail Recesses

Many articles and books speak of producing a dovetail recess in the base of a bowl by scraping with a skew chisel.

I don't like doing this, for two reasons. Firstly, the skew is far too noble a tool to be abused thus, its edge and long point needing constant attention to keep it sharp under normal use, let alone when being deliberately blunted in this way.

Secondly, the shoulder of the skew will

destroy any recess wall while the point is trying to reach down into the corner of the work (see fig. 77). Much better to make up a tool similar to that shown in fig. 78, but ground to a skew end. Round silver steel rod, or even an old round blade gouge which has been ground beyond its flute, will do admirably for this work.

77 Not this way

The great advantage of this tool over the skew is that its shoulder will clear the recess walls whilst working, the tool having a smaller diameter than that of the recess.

I use the tool in fig. 78 for the inside recess of small boxes and for the same wall clearing reason. But here the cutting edge is ground at 90° to the blade.

Another way of producing a recess was one which I came up with some time ago, when I was faced with the problem of holding 3/8″ thick by 6″ diameter discs on the lathe so as to decorate one face.

The face had to be solid and so I couldn't use a woodscrew chuck. I ended up grinding the parallel shoulders off a dovetail router cutter, holding the bandsawn discs in a jig and doing the operation on my overarm router.

A pillar drill might be persuaded to serve if your overarm router is at the mender's.

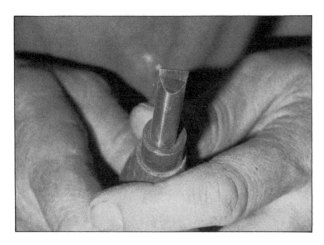

78 *Scraping rod*

8·17 Tool Handles

I have already touched on tool handles in chapter 4·1, but a couple more points are worth making.

First of all, the shape of the handle. I think that if the tool is long and/or heavy, then it should be fitted with a handle which should be compatible.

For instance, a 1″ wide skew, used on a planing cut would benefit from a handle which is longer than that of, say, a parting tool (see fig. 79).

Likewise a 1.5″ wide heavy duty scraper should have a handle which is wide enough, close behind the ferrule, to allow the turner a good solid grip, without risk of the tool flexing in use. (See fig. 79.) But extra length such as is

79 *Skew, scraper and parting tool*

found on the skew chisel is a waste of timber, and also of space in the tool drawer.

The parting tool handle should be long enough for two-handed use, but nothing like as long as the skew handle or as fat as the scraper handle.

Sets of handles, therefore, make for a nice neat package in the tool shop window and the presentation box, but how much more satisfying it is to make and use your own individually-sized handles for each one of the extra unhandled tools which you buy to increase the range of your set.

And the shorter handles can be made from any suitable, split-free timber. My tool trays boast afrormosia, ash, beech, oak and pine, plus some unidentifiable whatever.

I know of one woodturner who has identified his handles with a felt tip pen code at the butt end, a quick search thereby showing what tool can be found at the other end.

It is also true, of course, that just because a tool has a long handle doesn't mean the handle must be held at its end at all times.

I often find myself working with two hands on the blade and the handle supported by my body.

8·18 Scrapers

Many turners decry the use of scrapers, whilst other people who own lathes seem to use nothing else.

I have heard recently of an evening class in one of our local colleges of further education, which boasts no less than six lathes.

To quote the instructor, "We only use

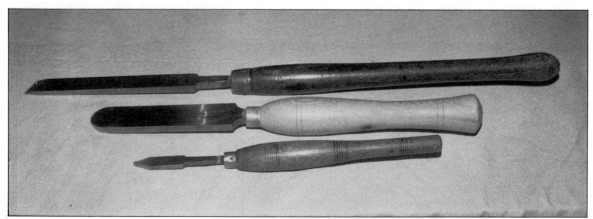

scrapers here because they are the best tools for turning''. I might be lucky enough to meet him one day and discuss the point.

Certainly though, there is a need for scrapers from time to time in spindle work, and more often when producing hollow ware.

There seems at the moment to be two principal methods of working with the scraper, sometimes depending upon the way the tool has been sharpened and sometimes actually dictating the sharpening method.

Neither method of using the tool requires the bevel to rub, which is just as well, because when a correctly ground scraper bevel rubs, people in the next street hear the resultant dig-in.

Whilst it is generally agreed that a scraper needs a burr, some tools work better with an almost burrless edge, the tool being presented to the work with its face almost at right angles to the work surface.

One instance of this is the inside of a narrow-necked box. In order to work inside the box with a small scraper, the tool should be presented flat on the tool rest and with the cutting edge almost up at right angles to the work surface, there being insufficient room through the neck of the box to allow the tool to be presented nose down, thereby allowing a burr to work satisfactorily.

A large open-topped bowl however, will allow a generous burr access to both its inside and, should it be needed, its outside.

The method of producing these burrs varies from turner to turner.

For instance, Frank Pain uses a 'ticketer' on some scrapers, depending upon the type of timber to be cut, whilst Peter Child uses the tool straight off the wheel, making no mention of the ticketer.

Both, however, grind the scraper with the tool 'right way up', whilst I grind the tool upside down (see fig. 20, chapter 5·5). My reason for this departure from the norm is that I think the resultant burr which I get from the wheel will comprise of more metal and less grinding wheel debris than the other method and should therefore last longer.

You will see from fig. 20 that I have a finger between the tool and the rest, so as not to wipe the resultant burr off on the tool rest whilst completing the grinding action.

And I do use a ticketer from time to time, to restore a worn burr. But then, I also invariably hone a gouge or chisel after grinding. Try out all the methods and make up your own mind.

A word of warning when contemplating the use of old files as scrapers. In case you have missed it, please have a look at chapter 4·4.

I repeat, a properly made scraper is much cheaper than an eye. And the only pain involved is to the pocket.

I have, on occasion, needed a hooked scraper (see fig. 80) – when making egg rings, for instance. Similar to captive rings, they are sometimes parted off in confined spaces which can be inaccessible to normal tools.

These hooked scrapers should be used nose down, as should all scrapers, otherwise they are liable to dig-in during use.

80 *Hooked scrapers*

9 Chucks and Other Holding or Driving Methods

9·1 Driving Centres

First, let's look at the humble driving centre, or claver as it used to be known.

A few years ago, the normal centre as issued with a lathe seemed to have two chisel points or prongs, but the four prong seems to be favoured nowadays.

Certainly I prefer the extra support for thin timber which the four prong centre gives, thus helping to counteract the tendency of the work to 'whip' on the lathe.

A selection of driving centres is shown in fig. 81. At 'a', we see the centre as it arrived from the manufacturer. It usually needs frazing. That is, the machine waste which is left on the centre should be removed with a small file, so that the timber is not restricted in its progress over the point and on to the prongs, or off them again, come to that.

At 'b', we see a centre which has been used and sharpened on a number of occasions, so that the point is now well proud of the teeth.

Time to rectify the situation by reducing the length of the point, so that the prongs can reach the timber again without putting too much strain on the lathe bearings.

Frank Pain shows a specially-ground file beind used for this rectifying work, but although he suggests a low lathe speed, I still prefer to use my engineering lathe.

At 'c', we find a centre which has been rejuvenated on the engineering lathe. You will notice that not only is the point protruding by no more than ⅛″, but the front of the prongs have also been squared and made the same length on the lathe. They are now ready for sharpening with a small file.

I occasionally find driving centre prongs on old lathes which have been sharpened to a

81 Selection of 4 prong driving centres

spear point. A reminder, no doubt, of the days when lathes could rotate in either direction.

The fourth centre is one which I had made specifically for large section turning between centres on my Coronet Major. The centre enables the corners of the square timber to clear the saddle when roughing out.

I have already dealt with centre finding and preparing the timber for spindle turning but I would like to make one quick point.

I don't like driving a centre point home before loading timber on to the lathe. In fact, I can remember doing it so few times over the last 18 years that I could almost say I never do it.

Only on extra long, and therefore heavier, work in the softer timbers, do I resort to the soft-faced mallet and certainly never the hammer, to gain a good purchase with the driving centre in the timber prior to turning.

I said in chapter 7·4 on awls, that I make a small diameter but deep centre hole in the face

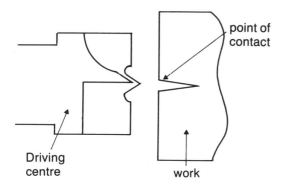

82 The long hole in the workpiece will guide the point of the driving centre

of timber to be turned. My reason for making such a hole can be seen in fig. 82. There is little resistance to the cone of the centre so that the prongs can reach the timber without undue strain.

I do have a selection of driving centres with different diameters, some bought as small centres and some modified as and when the need arose.

It is often useful to have a centre which is just below the size of the pin which may have to be turned on to the end of a chair leg for instance.

9·2   Tail Centre

The rotating or live centre made a great impact on the woodturning scene, but there are good centres and bad ones.

I have had some live centres which have not lasted any time at all, in fact one of them was decidedly 'graunchy' whilst it was still in the maker's grease.

The longest lasting centre which I have had to date was one which was made for engineering use.

Their life span does, however, depend upon how much work, of what type, is demanded of them. As one manufacturer said to me recently, "When we say our centres will last for a lifetime, we are speaking of ordinary turning. Two years of your kind of long and heavy work would be a lifetime for some people''.

My advice is to try another source if you find your rotating centres to be faulty.

Test it by holding the centre in one hand and the arbor in the other hand and then rotating one of them slowly, feeling for any resistance to the smooth flow which should be present.

You might even decide to change the bearings yourself if you think that the device is out of any guarantee time.

9·3   The Woodscrew Chuck

When I first started turning way back in 1966, my first woodscrew chuck was part of the power tool lathe attachment which I had conned my wife into allowing me to buy.

I still have the chuck (see fig. 83) and I now use it when I need small knobs with narrow holes.

83 Woodscrew chuck from a power tool lathe attachment

The chuck originally took a No. 6 woodscrew but I bored it out to accept a No. 8 as well, and it will even accept a parallel shank twinfast screw. I use it in the Handy Collet chuck, at one time made by Craft Supplies Limited of Derbyshire.

There are a number of different models of the versatile and relatively cheap screwchuck available nowadays. The Coronet 1½″ screwchuck is shown in fig. 84, but they can all be made more versatile with one or two simple additions.

First the wooden washer, or packing piece (see fig. 84). The counter-bored face should be against the work piece when the chuck is in use. This is to ensure that any waste wood which comes out of the work piece hole during

84 *Coronet 1½" screwchuck with packing washers*

loading, has less tendency to be trapped between the two faces, causing eccentricity.

This washer can do three things. Firstly, it controls the screw protrusion through the front of the chuck. It is often easier to fit such a washer than to re-adjust the screw. Removal of the washer will also sometimes allow a second chance to complete some work where the thread has been stripped first time round. Or do you never have dig-ins?

Its second function can be that of a sizing guide. The parting tool cut stopping just before the washer is found means that one less set of callipers is needed.

The washer's final use can be as an extension of the supporting face of the screw chuck.

This is achieved by using a washer which is larger in diameter than the face of the chuck. It is surprising how much extra support can be gained for a wider workpiece by using a washer as little as 1" larger in diameter than the chuck it is fitted to.

Most of the washers which I use are made from ply – normally 9mm, but it depends upon what my wealthy friends are throwing out.

I remember a job I did some years ago when the woodscrew chuck came into its own (see fig. 85). These were some finials which were to be turned, with a sharp edge at the end which was to fit on to the curtain pole.

The advantages of my method were that I could drill first and then having loaded it on to the lathe, turn the blank. I could turn right down and into the wooden packing piece

85 *Woodscrew chuck*

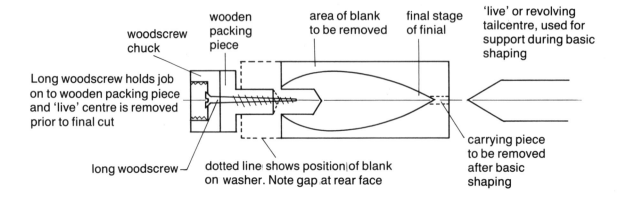

without losing any drive. I could also remove the carrying piece as a final operation. And all on the same setting.

One final bone of contention. I often see illustrations of knobs and similar items being turned between centres or 'gang turned' in one long strip.

This is said to be quicker than making the knobs individually as the lathe is only loaded once.

However, by the time the turner has overcome the whipping action of slender work, separated each of the knobs with a saw and then cleaned up the saw marks, the knobs might just as well have been made individually on the screwchuck in the first place.

Or even done individually between centres. See chapter 16·4 .

9·4 Bungs

One of the principles of spindle turning is that if a central hole is required in the finished work, the hole is usually drilled first and then used for location for the turning operation.

The advantages of this method of working are that it is usually easier to hold a square section than a round section for the drilling, and also that if the hole were drilled after turning, and the drill was not central or ran off for whatever reason, then concentricity would be lost.

So then, we have a hole at either or both ends of the work. How do we effect a drive when there is nothing for the point of a normal driving centre to make contact with?

The counterbore tool is the usual answer, of course, but it is possible to use other devices as well. First though, the counterbore. (See fig. 86.)

Provided the hole which has been drilled is either ¼″ or ⁵⁄₁₆″, then standard counterbore tools are available, as shown at 'a'.

What though, if the hole is larger than the standard sizes?

Just a little larger and with not too many pieces to do and the problem can be resolved by wrapping adhesive tape round the central boss to fill the gap. However, on long runs of work or larger holes, it is usually advisable to have made up an insert which will fit both the

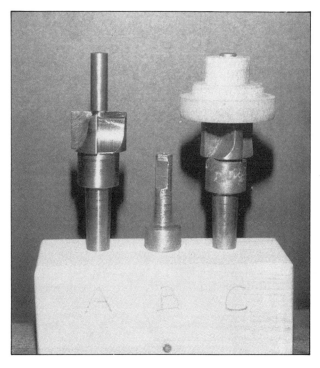

86 *A selection of counterbores*

hole and the counterbore, such as can be seen at 'b'. Metal inserts will obviously outlast wooden ones but if you can't find an engineer, ask around for the nearest woodturner.

When the hole to be used for location is larger than the diameter of the counterbore tool itself, then an adaptor will be needed. (See 'c'.)

This device is made to locate at the outer edge of the hole in the work and can be driven by a standard counterbore or even made to fit into a chuck. The drive, usually friction, can be helped by a strip of emery cloth glued to the driving surface, or even by sharp-headed pins. The beech bung in fig. 86c has three diameters and it is the middle one which locates inside the workpiece, the chamfer helping with this location.

The tailcentre can have similar adaptors made up for it, should a hole diameter exceed that of the rotating centre.

I have even fitted ferrules to some adaptors, to give them extra support on large batches of work.

So much then for larger holes. What about locating in small holes?

Some time ago, a self-taught woodturner

friend of mine spent a few days in my work-shop and we bounced ideas, and then friendly insults, off each other.

One of the things which John Sanders was doing was impossible in that he was turning between two 'vee' centres. ''I do it, Reg, because no one told me I couldn't''. And John is by no means the first person to have voiced that particular piece of philosophy.

John's findings were that although the drilled blank stopped rotating if too heavy a cut was attempted, or the tools were not sharp enough, access was gained to all the outer surfaces of the timber, in this case, light pulls.

I tried to improve on John's idea by using a wooden centre to drive with, so as to be able to cut into it with a tool, get a crisp edge on the work and yet not destroy the cutting edge of the tool.

I found however, that I couldn't get the same drive with this method, and also, when the wooden drive centre burned due to the work stopping, the burn mark was transmitted to the workpiece.

I now do light pulls as John does them, using a sharp-edged and narrow scraper to clean up at the driving centre end (see fig. 87), then

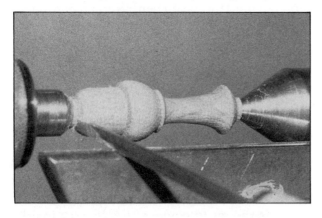

87 Driving from a 'vee' centre and cleaning up with a sharp-nosed scraper. Yes, it is oak.

reversing the work and repeating with the same tool. This means that I am not scoring an expensive live centre.

John also did interesting things with ring centres, the advantages being that a ring centre drive leaves a much more acceptable mark in the base of a workpiece than does the normal four-prong centre.

I do use the wooden bung principle of work driving when making thimbles.

A taper drilled hole – I used a ground down flat bit to produce the first ones, but now have a three flute router cutter which was specially made for the job – will fit on to a chuck held bung (see fig. 88).

88 Thimbles. Drilling a tapered hole to fit driving bung

The advantage here is in timber saving, an important consideration when dealing with exotics. A 1¼″ length of timber will produce a 1″ long thimble.

The wooden drive can also be used on solid end work, such as lace bobbins (see fig. 89). I prefer chuck held drives, usually just the body and the ring of the chuck holding the wooden driving device, but wooden bungs can also be made to fit into the jaws, depending upon size and type of chuck, size of available timber, etc.

89 Lace bobbin drive with yew blank

It is also possible to make up bungs with taper surfaces, usually No. 1 morse taper, which will fit straight into the headstock spindle of the lathe, so it is not vital that you have a chuck before you explore this interesting area of work holding.

I prefer to use the denser timbers for work holding duties, possibly because I am quite often dense myself, but an argument could be put forward in favour of softer wood, so as to avoid any chance of marking work surfaces.

9·5   Chucks

There are a confusing array of work holding chucks available nowadays, each one said to be better than its rivals.

I use a range of chucks, having no all-time favourite.

Some chucks offer a greater range of modes, others offer greater accuracy within a limited range.

My only advice to potential purchasers is to look hard at what is a constantly changing market, ask other users and then buy from an established manufacturer one of the equally well-established chucks offering a range of accessories which can be purchased as extras when the need arises.

My first three chucks, other than the humble woodscrew chuck, are no longer made, all having been incorporated into one 'all can do' chuck, the Craft Supplies Precision Combination Chuck (see fig. 90).

The versatility of a good chuck is limited only by the ingenuity of the turner.

For instance, one of the now obsolete chucks which I use quite often is the Craft Supplies Handy Collet Chuck, which used to boast a range of cast alloy jaws.

These jaws came in three hole sizes and each set of jaws had four pieces.

I purchased spare jaws and modified them to hold a range of squares (see fig. 91).

I also use the body and ring to hold some of the range of driving bungs detailed in the previous section.

The body and ring of the chuck can also be used for holding actual work, as in fig. 92. Here a packing piece is used between the workpiece and the chuck body, so as to cut down on the size of the waste.

It would also be possible to make up wooden jaws for the chuck to suit specific sizes of square or round timber.

Another of the obsolete chucks, which, incidentally, does have a modern counterpart, is the Craft Supplies Spigot Chuck.

This is, like the equally slim Handy Collet Chuck, a useful bung holder, except that with

90 Craft Supplies Precision Combination Chuck, Henry Taylor Masterchuck and Coronet Collet Chuck. Each one has a whole range of accessories.

91 *Method of holding square timber in a Handy Collet Chuck*

92 *Handy Collet Chuck by Craft Supplies Ltd*

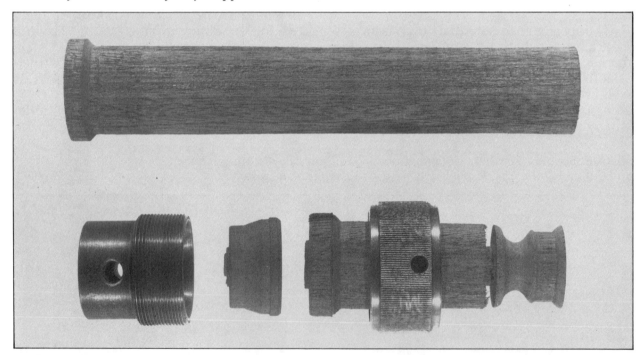

the spigot chuck I use the jaws to grip the bung. (See fig. 93.)

Also in fig. 93, you can see a two-part jaw set which I made up to suit a specific size of dowel. The jaws are held together in use by an elastic band.

Another well established and versatile chuck is the Coronet Collet Chuck (fig. 90) which offers three different modes, they being Collet, expanding jaw and centrifugal spigot.

New work holding devices are coming on to the market all the time and the latest one, at the

93 Craft Supplies Spigot Chuck

moment of writing, is the Roy Child Master Chuck (see fig. 90).

The great advantage of this particular chuck is its ability to accept a whole range of user-made jaws, each set being capable of gripping either internally or externally, or sometimes even both.

I repeat, the versatility of a good chuck is limited only by the ingenuity of the turner.

One final word on chucks. Far more skilled turners than I, use three and four jaw engineering chucks to hold wood. I don't like the principle, on grounds of safety. A momentary lack of concentration can cost a knuckle full of skin, and possibly even bone. Also a more positive grip on the timber will be achieved with one of the custom-made chucks, resulting in less likelihood of losing the work should a dig-in occur.

Having said all that, I have had occasion to hold small diameter dowel in a Jacob's type chuck before now, and have achieved this without any excessive squeezing of the timber by using a short length of metal tubing, the inside bore being compatible in size with the dowel diameter. A longitudinal saw cut in the tube allows it to close on the timber when gripped in the chuck.

9·6 Stuck In?

On occasions I have found problems in removing centres, chucks etc., from the lathe, particularly if they have been in place in or on the spindle for some time.

I prefer to use the thread protector on my Coronet lathe spindles, as it also helps in extracting tight centres, but if a centre which has stuck firmly were filed to accept a spanner or drilled for a tommy bar, extra leverage could be obtained on the centre.

When chucks or other threaded devices show a reluctance to give up their new found positions, it is usually the two flat faces, one at the rear of the chuck and the other one on the lathe spindle, which are causing the problem.

Some spindles have left hand threads, so first make sure you are not adding to the problem by tightening rather than loosening the chuck. I know it's a daft thing to say, but it wouldn't be the first time that mistake has been made.

An overnight soak in release oil will usually sort out any problems which tommy bars and pin spanners alone find impossible.

Tommy bars can be made up from old screwdrivers and should be kept near to the point of use, possibly in a drilled hole on a shelf or bench.

Whilst I don't like the use of pipe wrenches, mole grips etc., to gain extra purchase, 'needs must when the Devil drives'.

Once the two faces have been persuaded to part company, they should be examined for the cause of the problem and cleaned up if necessary. Care should be taken in this cleaning operation, so as not to affect any subsequent fit. It is sometimes a good idea to introduce a thin machined washer between the two surfaces, as this will give two sets of locating faces, and consequently two chances of overcoming any subsequent problems. Even a fibre washer would help.

Frank Pain shows a useful device for the removal of work which is stuck on a woodscrew chuck, but it could be that the use of a thin ply washer as suggested in chapter 9·3 would help over come this problem as well.

10 Drilling

10·1 General

This is a boring chapter . . . (Get it?!)

Basically there are two machines which I use for making round holes in wood: the lathe and the drill. There are advantages and disadvantages in both methods . . .

However, before we look at the machines in any detail, let's look at a few general points common to both.

I have already said that it is better if possible to drill before turning, because square stock can be held more easily than round. It is also better for reasons of concentricity. (See chapter 9.)

Occasionally though, I do some drilling after turning, when making table lamps, for instance. Whilst most of the drilling is done

prior to turning, I often leave the side hole for the flex until after the basic shaping. This enables me to look at the exposed grain and then to choose which should be the front of the lamp and which the rear.

Also, it does mean that care must be taken in drilling this final hole, so as not to damage the outer surface of the lamp when the drill makes it entry. However, slight disruption of a surface can usually be cleaned up on the lathe again afterwards.

Another example of drilling at least after the wood is loaded on to the lathe is in making twig pots. (See fig. 94.)

Here, the blank has been loaded on to a woodscrew chuck, the face trimmed with a spindle gouge and the tool rest set at right angles to the bed.

The spindle gouge is used to bore into the blank, taking care not to go so far in that gouge and screw meet.

94 *Boring with a gouge*

More usually however, drilling is done with a bit of some kind. When using either flatbits or twist drills, I often make specific modifications to the tools. Read on: –

10·2 Twist Drill

First, a word about the humble twist drill. The drill, when bought, usually has a cone point, which is fine in metal, but tends to disrupt the outer edge of the hole when working in wood.

A carefully-ground point and two wings will give a much cleaner entry hole in the work (see fig. 95). I do this modification with a grinding wheel, holding the bit in my hand and guessing the angles. Practice makes, if not perfect, then at least acceptable.

Standard sized wood bits are available from specialist suppliers, of course, but I usually find that the size I need is non-standard, and so the local ironmonger comes in handy. He has a good range of engineering drills.

96 *Flatbits*

95 *Modified twist drill*

10·3 Flatbit

Now to the flatbit. Fig. 96 shows a selection of these.

A standard flatbit is shown in fig. 96A. This bit should never be withdrawn after drilling a hole, until both it and the timber is stationary, as the bit relies upon its point location in the hole to support the two wings. The only exception to this rule is when the workpiece is held

securely in some mechanical device, such as a 'nippy' vice, which is itself secured to the drill table (as seen in fig. 97a). Even then, withdrawal of the bit after drilling should be as quick and as smooth as possible.

97a *A 'nippy' vice*

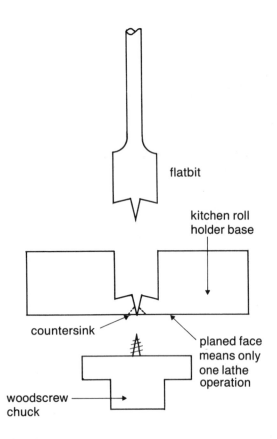

97b *Flatbit and woodscrew chuck*

When it is known that deep holes are not going to be needed from a specific bit, I usually shorten the shank of the larger ones, so as to cut down on the chance of problems with chatter when withdrawing the bit after drilling.

The standard bit can be used to produce both a hole and the location for a woodscrew in one operation, such as in fig. 97b, when making bases for kitchen roll holders etc.

The bit is set in a pillar drill so that its point just protrudes through the lower face of the work. The resultant small hole is countersunk so as to avoid any displacement of timber when the base is loaded on to the woodscrew chuck. The standard flatbit can also be used in counterbore operations, producing the larger of the holes. The locating hole made by the centre of the bit gives a start to the smaller diameter bit, which should be a cone-shaped twist drill, otherwise problems in starting the hole could be experienced.

Fig. 96B shows a flatbit which I have ground specially for counterboring pepper mills, table lamps and the like. The short shank cuts down chatter, the larger diameter is the standard 1½″ and the ground down section gives 1″ diameter, which just takes the counterbore tool that I use to drive table lamps.

One final use of a modified flatbit can be seen in fig 96C.

Here the ⅞″ diameter bit has a very short point. I use this bit to produce shallow holes in discs so as to grip inside them with small diameter jaws for my 6-in-1 expanding collet chuck.

An alternative to locating in the parallel hole left by either a flatbit or a Forstner bit is to grind off the nibs which are sometimes found on a dovetail router cutter and produce an angled recess in the rear of flat work, using either pillar drill or router. (See fig. 98.) The workpiece would, of course, have to be jigged for the drilling operation.

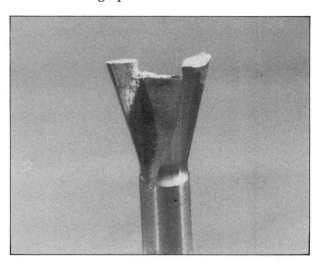

98 *Router cutter*

10·4   Lathe

Now to look at drilling on the lathe.

The first great advantage of horizontal drilling is that the shavings will usually fall away and not interfere with the subsequent location of the next workpiece.

The second advantage is that the option is open to rotate either the timber or the bit, depending upon the work being done.

A third advantage to a lot of turners will be that they don't have a pillar drill anyway!

When I am drilling work which is to be held between centres, such as a table lamp, I usually work between centres from the start.

Having found and marked the centre at each end of the work, I counterbore first of all with the flatbit shown in fig. 96b. The blank is located on, and held against, the tailcentre and then holding the blank with one hand and winding the centre with the other hand, the counterbore is produced. The lathe is switched off before the wood is withdrawn from the bit – (the lathe switches are at knee height, remember? Chapter 3, if you missed it) – and then a short $5/16''$ diameter twist bit is used from each end, in the same manner, except that the lathe can now be left running.

Finally, a long $5/16''$ diameter bit is used from each end until the two holes meet up. It may sound a bit long-winded, but some of my lamps are 18" or so high, making it more difficult for the holes to meet in the middle, so the long bit needs all the guidance it can get.

I don't use a morticer attachment or any other side locating device for this work as, until now, I have made lamps from assorted sizes of timber, twenty or so at a time, which would mean constant adjustments to any mechanical holding device.

If I get a shipping order for table lamps of all one size, it would then be economic to use the morticer attachment. Furthermore, if the blanks are of varying dimensions and very long, then it would be worth purchasing a suitable long hole boring kit.

I do have a morticer attachment for my second major lathe (fig. 99). It is an excellent device for repetition drilling on standard size stock but, like all such machines, it can produce attacks of earache, and so earmuffs should be worn.

Back to the lathe . . . and a couple of useful tips when drilling.

Firstly, tool rests can be set as depth stops if swung at right angles to the bed and then made to foul the drill chuck in its advance into the rotating stock (fig. 100).

The second tip is also a depth stop device, in

99 Drilling blanks with morticing attachment

100 *Tool rest depth stop*

a way. When using a woodscrew chuck to hold a rotating piece of work the tailcentre should be wound out fully before loading the work on to the screw, so that it detaches itself from the lead screw inside the barrel.

The tailstock assembly is then advanced along the bed so that the drill is well short of the screw. The position of the tailstock is now marked on the bed – I clamp the spare saddle to the bed, up against the tailstock.

The tailcentre is now wound back into the stock and the stock withdrawn along the bed.

Provided the spare saddle is not moved from its position on the bed, the drill can't now hit the woodscrew whilst the woodscrew chuck is being used for any repetition work which involves drilling holes.

10·5 Pillar Drill

Next in this boring chapter on drilling comes the pillar drill.

I have made a number of jigs for use with this machine. Fig. 101 shows some of them. Fig. 102 shows an early jig, now modified. The base is from scrap ply. It is also loose so that when the drill has broken through the work and into its face a few times, a new area can be easily found.

Finally, the jig can be seen to be held on to the drill by the use of 'G' cramps.

I now use the quicker method of holding jigs, as shown in fig. 103.

The advantage here is that I have an infinitely variable locating system, which is quite solid in use and quicker to set up than 'G' cramps, which have to work on the cross webbing found under most drill tables.

I also use a drill press vice for some work holding, and have fitted an auxiliary handle to it for quick action on repetition work (fig. 97a). The two part handle is held in place by the ubiquitous M6 roofing bolts, using wing nuts and washers. This makes the handle adjustable to any position through 360°.

101 *Selection of drill jigs*

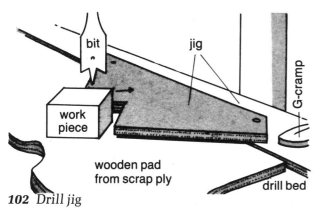

102 Drill jig

103 Wing nut, roofing bolt and ply washer

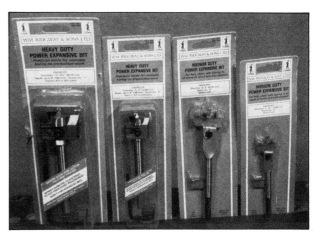

104 Ridgeway power bits

designed to pull themselves into and through wood at their own speed and also with the consequential lack of directional control. Try to force the pace with higher revs. and they will snatch and jam.

Remove the screw thread with a file, leaving just the point, and they will not draw themselves into the wood. Instead, they need a push from behind. This sometimes causes them to flex – again with subsequent loss of control.

And speaking of loss of control, it was drilling problems which finally persuaded me to invest in my long bed lathe.

Two-part newel posts with out-of-true sockets tend to have a drunken look when assembled.

10·6 Problems

Just to round off this chapter on drilling a couple of things to watch out for . . .

The first pitfall – and it's one of the few I did manage to avoid – is that you should not use an expanding bit, designed for a hand brace, in a power tool. It is likely to 'come from together' as my old Dad used to say, jam up in the hole and cause some embarrassment to fingers! Better to invest in one of the expanding bits made for machine use, such as the Ridgeway Power Expansion bit, available at the time of writing in four ranges of size (fig. 104).

The second way of contracting 'ooh, nasty' when drilling (and I still have the scar), is to use a long bit with a lead screw, at a fast speed. Machine bits which have these screws are

11 Repetition Turning

11·1 Introduction

Once basic knowledge and skills have been acquired, making something on the lathe is not particularly difficult. The fun starts when some sadistic person says that they want another one like it.

The first turning student I ever took came out to my workshop for a number of weekly sessions, each of two hours' duration.

He quickly progressed from basics and the projects got progressively more complex.

Finally he asked "Am I ready for a time-glass yet?" We decided that he was, and the end caps were completed without too many copying problems.

"Now Eric", I said, "We need the spindles. You can make the first one as elaborate as you like, but don't forget, you need another two like it."

"I've been thinking about that all week" he replied. "I want a straight line!"

Certainly, making more than one of something can be both technically difficult and also boring, but it is a skill well worth acquiring.

Members of the public often ask me if I don't get tired of making the same things all day when I am doing batch work.

I tell them that repetition turning is dull, boring, soul-destroying and rent-paying.

Most self-employed craftsmen need the 'bread and butter' work which pays the bills and therefore allows time for doing the more interesting, if sometimes less lucrative 'specials'. And anyway, working with timber means that there are usually a few pieces in the batch which require special attention.

11·2 Profile Gauges

Judging by the books and articles I have read on turning, the use of profiles is at least quite common, if not actually vital.

In fact, I don't use profiles when checking for consistency within a batch, for two reasons.

Firstly, it takes too long to make up an accurate profile in the first place, and if it is offered to the work in the lathe as a check, then the lathe has to be switched off first, otherwise the profile soon changes shape.

Secondly, profiles seem to demand the removal of thousandths of an inch in order to shut out the thin gleam of daylight, when in fact the material we have chosen to work with is almost certainly going to move for most of its finished form life anyway.

What then do I use, if not a profile gauge? I use a combination of pin sticks and callipers.

11·3 Pin Sticks

As I have already gone into the use of pin sticks in great detail in chapter 7·5, I shan't repeat myself as to their use. However, a couple of thoughts on their construction could be of interest.

I tend to use good quality birch ply, having access to generous offcuts of 9mm and 12mm thicknesses. The more pins the ply has to take, the greater the chance of splitting, so when two pins are close to each other, I usually put them into adjacent layers or seams, thereby spreading the load.

When a single pin stick is used on a long length of rotating timber, such as a staircase spindle, it has a tendency to get down between tool rest and timber. This problem is aggravated if the stick doesn't offer much of a hand hold in use and so I avoid sticks which are too narrow.

11·4 Cradles
(See also 17·3)

Having decried the use of profile gauges, I must admit to using a cradle at the rear of the headstock, the function of which is to support a sample of what I am turning. (See fig. 105.) It is very useful to have within sight a reminder of what the finished work should look like, whilst actually producing it.

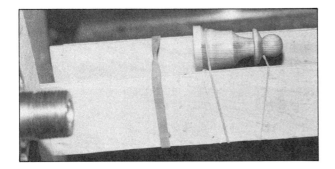

105 Pattern cradle

106 'Pocket money' products

This cradle device can take many forms, depending principally upon the size of work. For instance, long balusters, legs, etc., I clamp to a shelf which also holds paper, awl and other tools which could get lost amongst the shavings.

It is an advantage if the sample is positioned in direct line with the workpiece. This way an immediate sighting can be taken, bead for bead, cove for cove, without the irritation of having to 'aim off'.

The sample, however, should not be placed so close as to restrict access to the work with callipers, paper, etc.

11·5 Offcuts

One of the many advantages of repetition work is that it will often yield lots of regularly sized offcuts.

Whilst these can sometimes be a pain, ingenuity can often turn them into an asset.

For instance, at one time, I had literally thousands of 3" and 4" lengths of ⅞" diameter dowel around the workshop, all offcuts from one of my 'bread and butter' jobs which came up regularly.

I spent some time in the winter, feeding them into my ever-hungry stove, having nowhere else to put them.

Then I started making 'cheapies' for the craft fair outlets (see fig. 106).

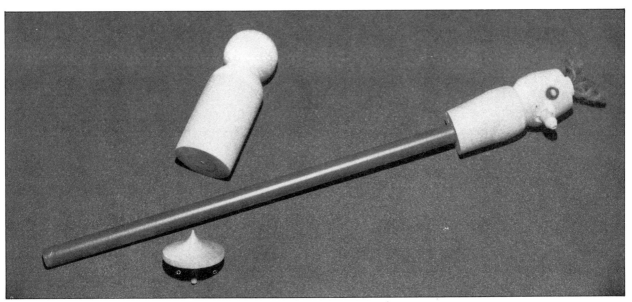

The skittles didn't sell too well – sets of nine, at something like 10 pence for each skittle being a bit beyond the range of pocket money – yes, I could have sold them cheaper than that, but anyone can work for nothing.

The finger spinners and woodpeckers sell quite nicely though.

Finger spinners are made from chuck held 4″ lengths, each one yielding four to five tops, whilst the woodpeckers come from the same stuff, but cross cut to 2″ lengths, drilled and held between driving bung and revolving centre. (See fig. 107.)

The woodpecker assembly is done at home, using slave labour. That is, younger members of the family who have negotiated a lucrative piecework rate.

I had made up some time glasses on a purely speculative basis for sale at craft fairs. One of these found its way into the hands of a cousin of mine who works for an advertising agency.

Cousin George designed a point of sale display round the glass, showed it to his boss and the outcome was that I got an order for 350 of them for use in jewellery shop windows, where they displayed watches. (See fig. 108.)

Whilst the profit margin on each unit was not as high as it had been on the original sample, that drop in profit was well worth while when you consider the quantity involved and the security of work which it brought.

11·6 Promotional Work

To round off this chapter on repetition work, I should mention a piece of good fortune which came my way a while back.

108 Turning 200 identical spindles is something of a challenge (opposite)

107 Woodpecker bung

12 Long, Slender Turning

12·1 Introduction

One of the questions which I am most regularly asked by the newcomer to turning is on choice of lathe.

The resulting discussion meanders slowly along a fairly well worn path, one of the usual viewpoints being the capacity between centres of the various makes and models of lathe.

The observation "I shouldn't think I would need to turn anything longer than about 2ft" draws from me the usual advice to measure the balusters at home, then add a couple of inches.

Most of the people who use lathes don't expect to be asked for work any longer than balusters, which are rarely longer than 42″, but 24″ is, to my mind, a bit on the short side. I suggest a minimum of 33″.

12·2 Steadies
(See also 7·7 and 8·2)

Next comes the question "What kind of a steady do you use?"

When I tell them that I use my hand, heads are shaken in disbelief, which was my own reaction when I first came across this statement during my early days of lathe exploration.

I told myself that there was no way I was going to touch that wood whilst it was revolving. I bought manufactured steadies which I didn't get on with. I made up book and magazine illustrated steadies which I didn't get on with. I invented roller bearing and rubber-tyred toy wheel steadies, which I didn't get on with. So I got on with the free hand support.

I soon learned not to grip too tightly. The hand is there to support the rotating work, not to try to stop the motor. The support is needed as close to the point of cut as possible, but on the opposite side of the timber to the tool, stopping it from taking its preferred path away from and then over the top of the tool.

I also learned to counteract the burning sensation in my hand by holding on to the bed of the lathe for a second or two. Try it! The mass of cool metal draws the heat from the hand.

I also learned that skin soon hardens.

A device which I came up with when turning walking sticks from 1¼″ × 1¼″ × 36″ was the 'ski'. (See fig. 109.) It fits the shallow gouge and protrudes over the top of the rotating wood, stopping the climbing tendency which is inherent in long, thin work.

109 'Ski' in use. The shallow gouge fits into a rectangular recess under the ski

I also find with slender work, that a bowl gouge, used well over on its side and taking 'bites' works better than the more usual 'long sweeps' of the roughing gouge. (See fig. 38, chapter 7·7.)

12·3   Extra Length Lathes
(See also 16·4)

No matter how long a piece of wood you can get between centres, some day you will be asked to do a job which is a couple of inches longer. My current capacity is 10ft., and it has happened to me!

The first time this happened to me, I employed lateral thinking. My lathe boasted the usual 33″ centres, whilst the work was 34½″ long.

A search for the shortest driving centre I had, got me an extra ¼″ of capacity, but I was still looking for 2″.

The ultimate solution was, in fact, to swap the positions of the tailstock and the lathe foot, making the rear of the tailstock flush with the end of the bed. This gained me the extra distance I was looking for. It sounds dangerous, but in fact the lathe isn't being put to much more strain than normal, providing the tailstock doesn't overhang the bed.

I once came up with a different solution to the same problem, where I needed to work on about 3″ at one end of a 4ft. length of timber. My longest lathe at that time was only capable of 33″ between centres, and so my youthful assistant held the live centre in his hand, braced himself against the wall and pushed. The job was completed just before young what's'isname got a second navel.

Should you decide on an extra length bed for a standard lathe, don't make the mistake of trying to fit extension pieces to the existing bed. The resultant loss of rigidity would make for poor work. Better to fit a longer, but complete bed.

My Coronet Major has an 11ft. bed, giving me 10ft between centres. When I ordered the bed from the factory, they had the foresight to send me an extra lathe foot as well, which I found I needed to stop vibrations in the bed.

It did give me the problem of where to put it in relation to the tailstock, but as I had a spare

110 *Underslung tailstock*

tailstock from the Combination Major, the problem was resolved. (See fig. 110.)

I still have to have two positions for the central foot, to ensure that either one or the other of the tailstocks can reach, whatever the timber length.

Owners of lathes with lift-off tailstocks, such as Arundel and Tyme, won't need to invest in extra tailstocks, but the longer beds should still be braced to cut down on vibration, even if the brace is nothing more than a suitably-shaped wooden block positioned between lathe and bench.

12·4   Turning Long Work

The longer work which I have done has usually been in one of the many species of pine. Fig. 111 shows the first 'tall order' which I completed on my long lathe. The columns were in Columbian pine, measured 6″ square by 8′9″ in length and weighed 56lbs.

I turned the work using a standard 4 prong driving centre, but I had hammered the centre well into the end of the blank, so as to give it plenty of 'bite'.

I sometimes use folding wedges on the saddle of the lathe at the headstock end, so as to align the centre hole with the driving centre before catching a bus to the tailstock end of the work in order to tighten up. (See fig. 112.)

I also pull the heavier lengths of wood round by hand just before starting the motor. This eases the starting load on the motor and also cuts down wear and tear at the driving centre end of the wood.

111 A tall order (Photo: courtesy of the 'Bromsgrove Messenger')

112 Folding wedges as height adjusters

One problem which I didn't anticipate, when turning the four long columns in fig. 111, was that on one of the blanks, the growth rings were closer together along one side than they were along the other.

This gave the rotating blank a weight differential so acute that, for a moment, I thought I had missed the centre when loading on to the lathe. Quick work with a large roughing gouge soon got the condition under control, but the experience gave me yet another factor to consider when timber is being selected for unusual jobs. My heaviest spindle job to date weighed 7¼ stones, and was from 8″ square Pitch pine, 8ft. long.

12·5 Problems with Long Turning

As with many aspects of turning, long work has its individual pitfalls, down most of which I have plunged headlong (sometimes more than once!) in the past.

As I have already said elsewhere in this book, a flat-nosed centre punch will often be better than a sharp, pointed one when marking the alternating hard and soft-grained timber which is so often used for these longer jobs. (See chapter 7·4.)

Something to be avoided on newel posts and the like is the use of a compensating timber to make up half of a post to a full post.

My experience in doing work for joiners and shopfitters is that when they want a half newel at the end of a landing, the principal timber is often supported by the use of a length of cheaper softwood, which make up the square, but which will be removed after the lathe work is completed.

This practice gives the turner one, and sometimes two, problems.

The first problem is that the blank is usually out of balance on the lathe, which can make for an exciting – if potentially shorter – life.

The second problem occurs when the glue line is on the centre line of the work, as there is a tendency for the lathe centres to split the work.

Better to use solid timber in the first place and rip the finished post after turning. The saving in labour would probably cover the extra timber cost, and you often end up with two half newels for the price of one.

I also get lumbered – sorry, burdened – with the problem of newels which have suffered the attentions of the morticer before they came to me. This can also cause balance problems.

In one extreme case I ended up sawing and fitting temporary tenons to compensate for the weight loss.

And one final point – this time regarding glue . . .

For all the work I do which needs glueing, I use a P.V.A. glue, which needs no mixing, has a long shelf life and is kind to tools.

Some laminations which I have had to deal with in the past have proved most unkind to cutting edges. "It's like planing bricks" someone once said to me.

12·6 Special Jobs

'Specials' is a title which I give to any jobs which are out of the normal run of work.

In my field of being a 'jobbing' turner, who will tackle anything within his capabilities, there aren't many specials.

However, I do get them. Jobs which are financially non-viable, but which are worth much in the barter market, are specials. One such was reported in 'The Great Mangle Roller Disaster', which I won't go into here, but a search through back copies of *Woodworking*

Crafts magazine (the forerunner of *Woodworking International*) will reveal all. I lost money on it, but I kept a timber merchant happy, and that proved worthwhile in the long run.

Another definition of 'special' might be jobs where the annual production could be counted on the thumb of one hand. Cabriole legs come into this category.

I turn them from North Sea sharkwood at evening talks, but this is just to show the principle, or to increase the awareness of an audience. These cheapies I throw away, as North Sea sharkwood is, in fact, the cheaper stuff which might otherwise have become fish boxes.

I also occasionally do an oval turning for the same sort of reason – that is, to entertain the public.

I expect most readers who need to do this sort of work are fully aware of the principles involved and so I shan't go into them again here.

If anyone is not aware of these principles, then Peter Child's book should be referred to (details in the bibliography).

Rings are fun things to turn. Whilst I haven't turned them in great numbers, they are a job which come up occasionally and as neither Child nor Pain mention them, I shall . . .

My method, I think as per Geoff Peters, is to fix a slightly oversized disc to the woodscrew chuck and produce three quarters of the section, as in fig. 113.

The work is now sanded and then reversed on the screwchuck and the final quarter is turned, the revolving ring being supported with the free hand during breakthrough to avoid any impromptu games of hoop-la.

A couple of wooden chucks could be made so that the work can be put back on the lathe for sanding. Alternatively, the Roy Child Master Chuck could be pressed into service.

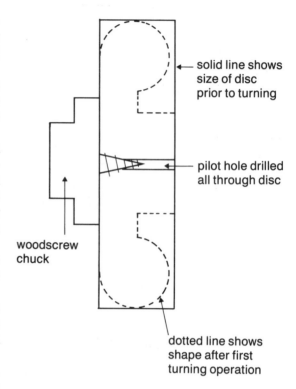

solid line shows size of disc prior to turning

pilot hole drilled all through disc

woodscrew chuck

dotted line shows shape after first turning operation

113 Turning a ring, stage 1 – the easy bit

13 Finishing

13·1 Introduction

To sand or not to sand, that is the question. (Sorry, Will.) In 1982 I wrote:

"One of the objectives which the turner should aim at is to do as little sanding as possible, relying on the finish from the tool.

However, I maintain that if, to achieve this, I have to spend more time sharpening tools than I would spend sanding a slightly rougher turning, then I would rather sand. Time is money.

Of course, too rough a finish from a blunt tool would require a lot of sanding, and even then possibly not be right anyway, so a compromise must be sought.

A finish from the tool which can be improved on with abrasive paper is my norm and I usually use 100 grit or 150 grit paper for the initial sanding."

That statement is just as true today as it was then, and most of the turners to whom I have spoken since 1982 have agreed with me.

13·2 Finish from the Tool

There are ways of achieving this better tool finish if sanding is to be kept to a minimum. Not all of these methods are practical under all conditions.

A lighter cut with a newly-sharpened tool is the commonest method, provided the penultimate cut didn't tear out any grain, which would leave holes in the finished work.

A slower feed with the newly-sharpened tool would also help in that you would get more cuts to the inch of traverse and greater burnishing from the bevel of the tool. This can be overdone of course, some timbers being prone to bruising and some tools being equally prone to loss of temper at the cutting edge.

Alternatively, a faster speed for the workpiece can sometimes be employed, in conjunction with the newly-sharpened tool.

13·3 Sanding

Before any abrasive paper is used on the work it is as well to finish as much of the turning as possible, as tools which are re-applied to surfaces which have been sanded will soon lose their edge, due to the fine particles of abrasive left in the work.

The advice to sand under the work is to be followed where possible, for two reasons.

Firstly, if you do lose the paper it goes away from you rather than towards you. Secondly, the dust goes in the same general direction as well. However, there are exceptions which prove the rule.

If I am sanding a long parallel or tapered section of work, I use the paper over the top in two hands. (See fig. 114.) This way, very little dust gets trapped between paper and work.

114 Overhand sanding

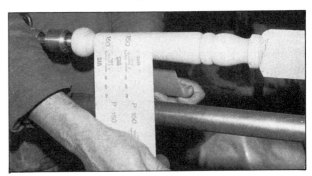

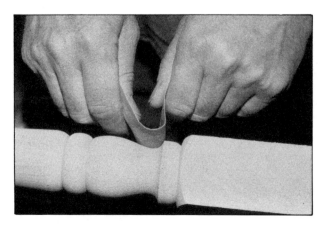

115 Sanding coves

Another exception is when sanding coves. (See fig. 115.) I make a loop of the paper and work from the front, watching the results from over the top of the lathe. The loop of paper must be kept on the move to avoid 'tramlines' in the work.

13·4 Problems

In my experience, abrasive paper is hell bent on self-destruction by attracting moisture. Indeed, it sometimes seems able to draw a drop of water all the way through a bucket of oven dry sand.

One way to dispel any small amounts of moisture is to keep the paper near the heat of a light bulb for a while prior to using it. Under severe conditions, I have been known to have a dozen or so strips of the stuff decorating the shade of my lathe lamp whilst I am working. The conglomeration looks not unlike a drying jellyfish!

One of the oft repeated pieces of advice is to pad out abrasive paper with shavings or steel wool when sanding. The suggestion is offered as a means of cushioning the work and keeping fingers cool.

Whilst I agree that it does both, I am also aware that my fingers are a good temperature gauge when in direct contact with the working paper. If my fingers are getting warm, how does the poor timber feel?

I do use both methods, but discourage students from using the sandwich principle until they are aware of the potential heat split

problems which can result in lack of thought or 'feel' for the wood.

On occasion, I find that I am working on a selection of different timbers, for instance when I am making lace bobbins.

I discovered the hard way that abrasive paper will take up the dust from rosewood, ebony and other dark timbers and distribute it amongst any lighter bobbins which follow, giving the finished product a most unhealthy appearance.

I now grade the selected blanks in order of colour and then start at the light end of the spectrum working on towards the infernal stygian gloom of ebony, the dust from which tends to get into more inaccessible places than engineer's blue.

13·5 Barrelling

I have in the past used a barrel rumbler when sanding lots of small components. (See fig. 116.)

In engineering, the shape of the barrel is very important, as is the choice of de-burring media. However, my barrelling work was not such an exact science. I used a rectangular box – because I had a rectangular box already made up – with flanges made from ply discs and old car fan belts as tyres.

The box was made to rotate at about 18 r.p.m., the drive being from a motor, through pulleys to a rubber hose ended roller, with an idling roller at the rear. This rubber to rubber effected a better drive.

My first experiments were based on the engineering principles and so I used old abrasive paper in with the work, but I found that any time I saved in this mass sanding was lost again in sorting out the work from the paper.

I ended up putting the work in on its own and found that with a load of no more than ¾ capacity, the 'thunderer' worked well. Should you decide to make a barrel, a frame which supports noise deadening blankets is a good idea unless, of course, you don't like the neighbours!

These barrels are also used to distribute sanding sealer but most of my industrial turning leaves the workshop with a sanded finish

116 *Barrel rumbler*

117 *Starting on the side grain*

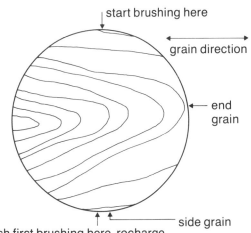

only, the customer preferring to apply his own finish to the completed article.

I enjoy this arrangement as wet lacquer and dusty atmospheres do not live happily together.

13·6 Brushing

On the occasions when I do use lacquer and it is to be applied to end grain (on a kitchen roll holder base, for instance) I always start the first coat on the side grain and work through the end grain area in one application (see fig. 117), recharging the brush when I get to the opposite face, and then continuing round the base to the starting point.

If the starting point is on end grain, it can often be seen as a dark line when the work is finished.

13·7   Matching Finishes

One final point on the subject of finishing: I do quite a bit of restoration work, replacing lost finials, knobs, etc.

When my customer is going to blend the new pieces in with the old ones and match the colour I give him a few offcuts of the replacement timber so that he can experiment with stains etc., before setting about the new component.

This gesture costs me nothing, and I am liable to get more work from the customer because 'I showed some thought'.

14 Producing samples and Working for Industry

14·1 Introduction

So often, when doing 'industrial' work, I am asked to copy existing designs which have been produced by someone else in the past.

First of all I try to find out why the customer wants to change his supplier. After all, it could be that there are some unpaid bills about and that credit has been used up with Bloggs Woodturning Ltd!

If I think that things might get out of hand I ask a trade protection association to check up on credit ratings, etc. – but more of that in chapter 21.

From the technical point of view, there should be no insurmountable problems in producing by hand what someone else has already made using the same methods, although this will sometimes mean a change of techniques, tool shape or whatever.

However, when work is new and the design is left to me, I try not to make rods for my own back.

14·2 Pitfalls

I have found in the past that I have created samples with little thought given to the time involved, only to find that they could not be reproduced in quantity, for a variety of reasons.

For instance, I have placed delicate little beads at the bottom of deep coves. I have spent too much time sanding to an extra fine finish. I have produced knobs with one continuous flowing surface. I have used timber which I couldn't buy for a reasonable price in sufficient volume for the production work. You name the clanger and I've dropped it!

First of all then, it is a mistake to spend time creating a pleasing shape which is too complex to reproduce economically. Always have the probable selling price in mind. Alternatively offer two samples – the cheap one to a specific price and the more involved (and therefore more expensive one) as an alternative. This gives the customer the final choice.

Secondly, try to incorporate some 'aiming points' into any design. By this I mean some features which allow the use of callipers at particular points. Fig. 118 shows what I mean. The knob at 'a' has three definite sizing diameters, making it an easier shape to reproduce than that at 'b'. I also think it looks better!

118 Built-in aiming points

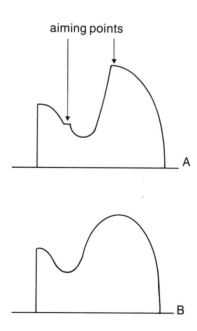

Finally, ensure suitable supplies of timber before committing yourself to long production runs of work at a fixed price. And if you can't guarantee the cost of the timber, don't guarantee the selling price.

Those are the three most common hazards in my own experience.

One further problem to be aware of is that of verbal descriptions.

I have in the past produced samples, based upon a conversation with a customer, only to find that his idea of 'medium oak' does not tally with mine, or our interpretations of 'traditional' legs are poles apart.

14·3 Drawings

I do like to work to a sample or at least a drawing, which has been supplied by the customer.

Copying a sample then should not have any great problems, but the same cannot be said of drawings.

A quick sketch from a customer (often on the back of a cigarette packet!) should be avoided. It could be open to a variety of interpretations.

Drawings from engineers often call for finished diameters on the job which assume that the work has come from bar material of that size, and not from standard sawn timber sizes.

For instance, a 2″ diameter finish cannot always be taken from 2″ sq. timber and, when pressed, the engineer will often say "Oh, 1¾″ diameter will be fine". But get it in writing if you can.

Architects are quite often similarly vague creatures. An architect is a bricklayer with a knowledge of Latin.

I rarely produce drawings for a customer, as I find it quicker to produce a sample on the lathe, having been given overall dimensions. Also things very often look entirely different in three dimensions.

On the occasions when I do draw out work before producing it on the lathe, I only draw one side. (See fig. 118.) This is quicker and easier than trying to get both sides of the drawing to look alike.

14·4 Timber

Quite often I am asked to work in timber which

has been supplied by the customer, and I am usually happy to do this as it means no timber bill for me.

The customer may himself make this suggestion so that the legs, knobs or whatever it is I am producing for him will match the furniture which he is making. However, whatever the reason, care should be taken before agreeing to the condition, as it can lead to problems.

A non-turner's idea of what can and cannot be turned is not always as accurate as it could be.

For instance, a blank of wood which has had a knot taken from one edge during sawing, is still going to be short-grained in the area of the knot.

A length of wood which has been cut extra long to allow for the split ends still has to revolve and is therefore not as stable as a shorter piece with no splits.

Finally, if a mistake is made by the turner, it has to be rectified at his expense. If he is using his own stock sizes of timber then his mistake is annoying but not necessarily costly. However, if timber is specially prepared by the customer, then it can be expensive to replace.

15 Gadgetry

15·1 Introduction

This chapter is dedicated to all the special tools which I have made up but which are not mentioned in any other sections of the book.

As with most turners working in isolation, some of my gadgets are new, some old ideas rediscovered and some probably generally accepted within the trade.

15·2 New Ideas

Woodturning is a popular hobby with thousands of people, many of whom try to bring new elements into the craft.

I was going to revolutionise the game when I first became interested in turning, way back in 1966. I was going to use wide form tools, ground to shape, hand held and pushed into the revolving wood. I thank whichever deity it was who dissuaded me from this potentially

catastrophic course of exploration into producing sharp splinters of flying wood and broken fingers.

However, I think I can lay claim to two innovations, the first of which is proof of the age old adage 'Necessity is the mother of invention'.

When turning recesses in lidded boxes (fig. 119), the shoulder of a parting tool or a skew scraper tended to destroy the wall of the recess whilst the tool point was working the angle at its base.

My solution to this problem was to grind a length of silver steel rod to the shape shown in fig. 78. This tool is used like a scraper and as it is of a smaller diameter than the recess it is working in, there is no fear of the wall being damaged during the critical sizing operation (see fig. 120).

A similar tool, ground to a skew end, could be used to produce the dovetailed recess needed in bowl bases prior to their fitting to expanding chuck jaws. And, of course, the tools can be made from those seemingly wasteful long tangs which are left when the new

119 Box with internal fitting lid

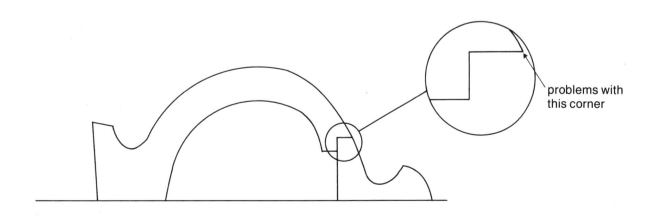

problems with this corner

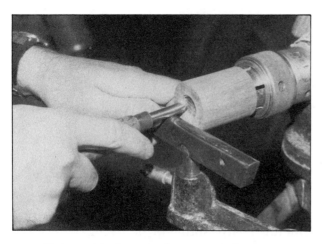

120 Sizing with the round scraper rod

style round section gouges have finally been ground down past the flute.

The second innovation which I can lay claim to is one which has been used in engineering for years. It is the gap gauge.

At the moment of writing, the first production gauges have been produced (fig. 121). My original gauge is shown on the left. The idea was offered to Nick Davidson of Robert Sorby & Sons Ltd., whose production gauge is shown on the right.

The gap gauge is filed to a standard size by the turner and then used instead of callipers.

A range of gauges covering standard sizes will be cheaper than the same number of callipers for repetition work. The gauges can be easily identified with a marking pen, they won't open out in use and when they do eventually wear, they can be re-filed to the next size up.

Of course, when being used for internal sizing the timber should be stationary.

15·3 'Re-invented' Ideas

The upside down parting tool has already been mentioned in chapter 8·1, together with my modifications. The earliest mention I have come across of this tool is in Holtzapffel and I suspect it will still receive a few modifications as time goes by.

Also worth mentioning amongst the re-invented gadgetry are the sizing fingers shown in fig. 122.

These are used instead of callipers, and not only do they give an indication of diameters, they also show where those diameters should be on the work.

The fingers are produced by Craft Supplies Limited.

121 Gap gauges

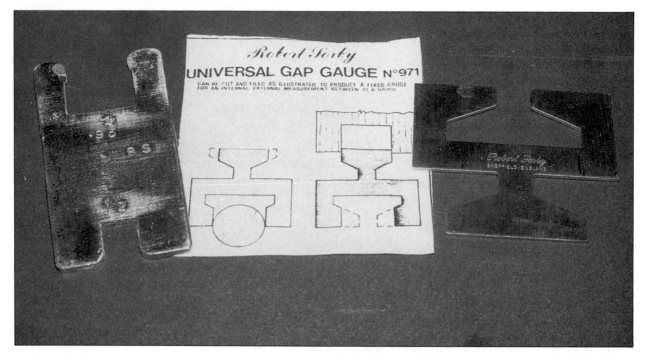

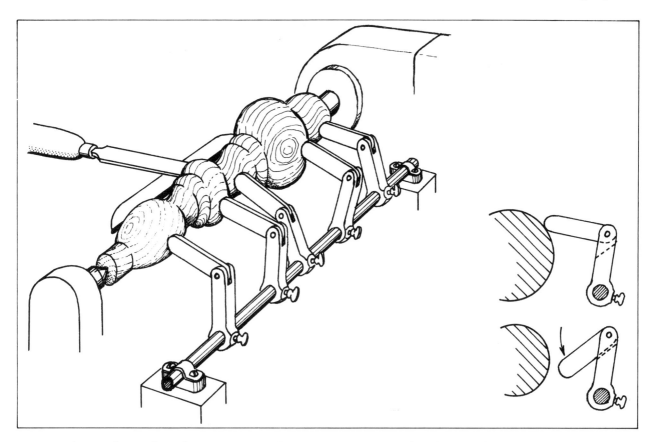

122 *Craft Supplies Ltd Craft Copying Attachment*

123 *Special tools come from many sources*

15·4 Generally-accepted Ideas

Not at all new, but still worth a mention, are the tools shown in fig. 123. These are a series of special tools which I have made up from a collection of broken foil and épée blades.

Whilst the steel is not the best for such use, I have a lot of broken blades about and it is a simple matter to fit a short length to a handle, grind the end to the required shape and thus add to the growing range of special small tools.

Old machine planer blades have been used in a similar manner, as have thick power hacksaw blades and even masonry nails.

Of course, care should be taken when using such tools, and if either heavy cuts or a lot of work are required of them, then it would be better to buy properly produced tools where available.

16 Tricks

16·1 Introduction

This chapter will be contentious! Some of the things which I get up to in my professional workshop would give some turners the screaming hab dabs, and cause junior factory inspectors to lick their pencils and dream of instant promotion.

'Dangerous' practices become safe in experienced hands, but practice in isolation.

One such dangerous activity is that of loading and unloading the lathe whilst it is running.

Obviously this time and power saving process can only be done if the conditions allow.

For instance, I usually employ the method when working between centres on blanks up to about 2ft. in length.

Frank Pain summed up the usual public reaction to this activity. When asked by a watcher if the wood hit him very often, the turner said, "No, usually just once".

Chapters 6·4 and 19·2 should be read by anyone planning ventures into this area.

16·2 Preparation

These three points are not connected specifically, but I can't think of any other collective heading!

First – and this is a repeat of something already said, but important enough to say again – have the stop button, or at least a cut-out button, at or near knee height so that if hands are busy averting potential disasters, broken windows and the like, the lathe can still be switched off with one of the lower limbs.

Secondly, in similar vein, take pockets off overalls if tool handles are likely to catch in them during cuts. In fact, remove any potential obstructions from pockets anywhere. A pocket full of coins contacted at the wrong moment can cause a design change at the lathe end of the tool.

Thirdly, I have found it useful at times to identify one of the chisel points on a driving centre, so that should work have to be removed from and then returned to the lathe, it can be replaced in the same position, thus cutting down on the chances of eccentricity. Fig. 124 shows what I mean here.

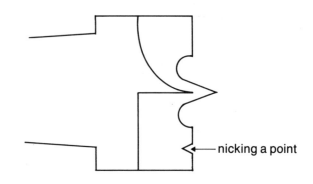

nicking a point

124 'Nicked'!

16·3 Design

As I have already said in chapter 13·2, it is easy to make a rod for your own back.

I once produced a few sample bases which were 6" diameter, ½" thick and decorated on one face with shallow rings.

I used a narrow half-round scraper for the rings, and whilst the samples were fine, I had about 10% rejects on the production batch

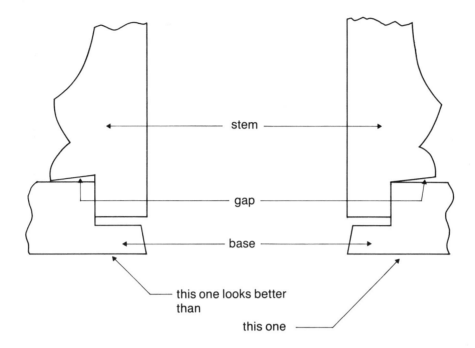

125 *Kitchen roll holder, stem and base fitting*

because some of the discs would not run in the lathe chuck with a true face.

This meant that the half-round decorative groove was wide at one side of the face and narrow at the other. The problem was overcome by changing to a narrow and parallel scraper, which gave a consistently wide groove, the varying depth of which, when it occurred, was not obvious.

Another design feature, not by any means new but worth mentioning, is to slightly relieve one of two faces which are to touch at a corner, on kitchen roll holders, for instance. Fig. 125 explains this in more detail.

Also on undercutting, I have found sometimes that when producing pins to which sharp-edged ferrules are to be fitted, a shaving is often cut from the pin during ferrule assembly. This shaving usually gets caught between the two abutting faces when the ferrule is finally fitted, and is unsightly.

To over come this problem, I make a very slight undercut at the base end of the pin so that any shavings will become detached and fall free, with a little assistance, before the final fit is achieved. See fig. 126.

126 *Getting a clean fitting ferrule on a handle*

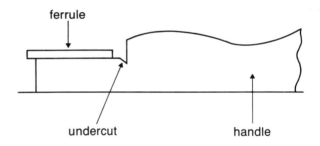

For years I have been making small knobs on a woodscrew chuck.

Now, where possible, I make them between centres. (See fig. 127.) The carrying piece at the tailcentre end can be taken off with a skew, after removal from the lathe, and a quick dab with fine paper will blend in any turning marks at the centre.

This only applies to work which has a sanded finish, but it is yet another time saver, allowing as it does for loading and unloading without switching the lathe off. Chapter 19·2 goes into this in more detail.

Finally, where possible, I often shape the

tailcentre carrying piece as shown in fig. 128, so that after sanding, it can be reversed, the cone section fitting into the gullet of the driving centre.

The advantage of this is that the work can now be re-sanded with the last grade of paper, the reversed direction of rotation giving a better finish. And provided you get the geometry right, you can do this without switching the lathe off.

16·4   Setting

When setting up for work which is thin, such as wheels, whizzers (fig. 129) and the like, I usually set the tailcentre at its maximum travel and then move the whole tailstock assembly along the bed of the lathe so that the two centres are just clear of each other. (See fig. 130.)

When loading, the handwheel is used to withdraw the tailcentre sufficiently, allowing the work access between centres. The handwheel is then tightened again, causing the work to be driven by the chisel points of the driving centre.

If the work now stops during a cut, the handwheel can be given a quarter turn, thus regaining drive to the work, but without fear of the two centres contacting each other.

127 Knob between centres

128 Reversible carrying piece

129 A Whizzer

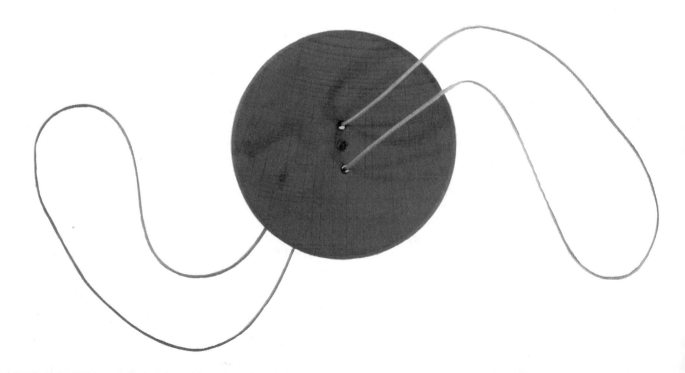

130 Point to point

As I have already said in chapter 12·13 I have coaxed extra distance between centres from a lathe by moving the tailstock to the end of the lathe and having the support bracket inside it.

This is not as dangerous as it looks. The tailstock doesn't – or at least shouldn't – rely on anything but its grip on the bed to stop it from moving along the bed. There should, of course, be no overhang of tailstock beyond the end of the bed.

When setting the tool rest for normal work on my single round bed lathe, I sight along the rear of the rest and align it with the lathe bed, rather than with the timber being worked.

This ensures a consistent alignment rather than one which might be affected by poorly centred or out of square stock.

Of course, I still spin the work by hand prior to switching the lathe on, to ensure work clearance with the tool rest or any other projections.

Some lathes have drop bars on their tool rest fixing screws and these are usually arranged so that the bar will drop out of the way when the screw is hard against the tool rest post. Sometimes, however, due to the configuration of the screw and banjo threads, the drop bar finishes in a horizontal position. When this occurs, an elastic band wound round the drop bar will prevent it from vibrating forward and into the rotating work, which can result in modifications of design to say the least.

An alternative method of adjustment which can also be applied to the fixed bar type screws, is to saw, file, grind or in some other way remove the end of the screw in order to achieve a better position for the handle. Brass pellets can be used in the threaded holes to adjust the final positon of the drop bar, as on some lathes, but if left loose, they would soon get lost. If you go to these ends, then either screw or glue the brass pellets to the end of the screw.

If the turning tools are sticking on the tool rest during use and the usual culprits – burrs on the tool rest – are not present, then wax the working surface of the rest. It is also a good idea to check that you removed all those nasty groove-making sharp corners from the blades of the factory fresh tools when you first took them from their wrapping paper.

You did stone the sharp corners, didn't you?

16·5 Working

I do like to hold the revolving work with my free hand, principally to deter it from vibrating and causing chattering marks on the finished surface. But there is another reason for getting to grips with the stuff. I am often given information which sight and sound can't detect.

I have discovered slight splits, small knots and narrow flats on the revolving timber because I am literally in touch with it.

Obviously the work needs to be round, or at least near round, before it can be handled safely.

Another way of checking for flats if you can't feel them during the actual cut, is to lightly hold the blade of the tool on the top of the rotating work and feel or listen for 'knocks'.

One of the most frequent problems which I encounter with students is that the flute of the gouge is restricted in some way, usually with a thumb, whilst the tool is cutting.

This fault results in a pile of shavings just behind the cutting edge, which can result in a clogged tool, pushing the tool away from the rotating work.

Better to keep the shavings path clear so that they can find their way down the flute and on to the floor.

Thumb or fingers can, in fact, often be used as a shavings deflector – thus keeping eyes, nose and mouth clear of debris!

Another natural tendency of the novice turner is to watch what the tool is doing at the point of cut, where the view is, in fact, obscured by the shavings.

Much better, once the cut has started, to watch the 'up' side of the rotating wood, where a much clearer image of what is going on can be seen. In the same way, learner drivers are discouraged from looking for the gear lever when out on the road.

Written advice on sizing cuts with the parting tool varies from turner to turner. Some say start the cut with a scrape and then lower the handle, allowing the bevel to rub, as this helps to cut down the 'spelch' or surface disruption on either side of the cut.

Others merely scrape with the tool all the way in, by holding it horizontally.

A third school seems to advocate the rubbing bevel to start, raising the handle to achieve the cut and then just pivoting on the tool rest, so that as the worked diameter reduces, the cut in fact becomes a scrape.

I feel that the cut should be a cut throughout and I follow the third school of thought except that, as well as raising the tool handle during the cut, I also advance the tool over the rest as the cut progresses. This means that I am working with the tool between 10 o'clock and 11 o'clock throughout the cut. (See fig. 131 and also chapter 8·8.)

Whilst it should be the aim of every turner to work with either hand – I'd give my right hand to be ambidextrous – there are times

132 Maximum support for both timber and tool

when I use the crosshands technique. (See fig. 132.)

This probably is not by any means new, but often of great use when pummels restrict the use of a steadying hand on long and slender work. As can be seen, the tool can be supported by the wrist of the steadying hand, during cuts.

I first started using this method of work steadying and tool holding when using the skew but I have found myself applying it to gouge work as well.

131 Parting tool advancing over tool rest during cut

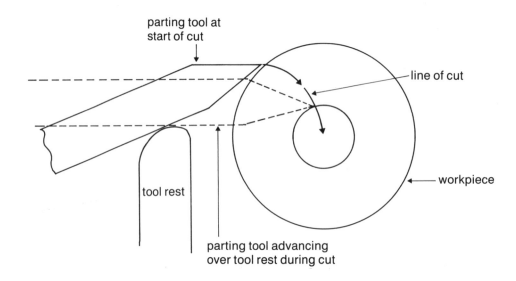

parting tool at
start of cut

line of cut

tool rest

workpiece

parting tool advancing
over tool rest during cut

16·6 General

Once again, a couple of useful ideas which I couldn't find a more suitable heading for.

I usually make my own ferrules for tool handles from offcuts of copper pipe which I 'came by' in the murky and distant past.

I recently bought a pipe cutter of the type used by plumbers (see fig. 133), and now I can produce ferrules which are square-ended rather than the hacksawn wedges which are to be found on some of my tool handles.

And to finish this chapter, I like to advertise when it costs me nothing. I usually do this by

134 Making my mark

133 Ferrule maker

A thin wad of felt between the work and the solid table will stop this damage to a waxed or lacquered face.

I use the top of my old cast-iron saw table as a support during stamping. Too flexible a support, or too thick a wad of felt, can result in a double image from the stamp, caused by the work bouncing during the stamping operation.

Metal stamps can be ordered from engravers who, in turn, can be found under that heading in the yellow pages telephone directory.

Special pieces such as boxes, translucent goblets, etc., can be signed with a fine, waterproof pen, a pyrography machine, or even a branding device, as appropriate.

fixing a label of some sort on to the craftwork, where possible.

However, a much more permanent mark can be made with a metal stamp. (See fig. 134.)

The stamping operation is usually done on the base of the work, but this occasionally damages the finished face of the work.

17 Shop-made Accessories

17·1 Introduction

Many, if not all, woodturners have got their own favourite 'gadgets'. These devices they have made up to get them out of a particular difficulty, to overcome a lack of skill, or to fill a gap in their range of tools.

Indeed, some of these 'indispensable' aids are so complex that the fun has been in their design, development and manufacture rather than in their use.

I am always aware of the danger of wasting ten minutes to save five. For this reason, most of the following ideas are simple in design and manufacture. They are not, however, without development.

17·2 Marking Out

Ply discs are a great help in marking out bowls from boards very much as a dressmaker uses paper patterns.

The discs are marked out with a compass from waste ply or hardboard and then bandsawn accurately. The centre can be drilled to take either a small bradawl or a plug (as in fig. 135) and the disc size is then marked with a broad felt tip pen.

It is useful to have more than one disc of each size, but this depends upon storage space, availability of offcuts and potential return in the saving of time compared with the time taken to produce the discs.

I use the fig. 135 variation of these discs when cutting waney edge bowl blanks on a bandsaw. (See fig. 136.) The blank is chainsawn to approximate size, and given a flat base.

A suitably-sized disc is placed on the waney edge, the centre marked and the blank drilled

135 Marking discs

136 Bandsawing to a circle

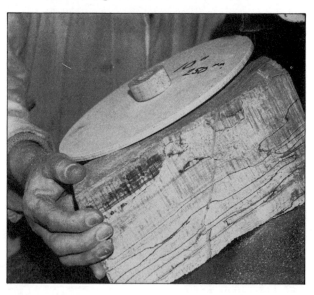

out to suit the pin chuck. Next the disc is held in place by a locating peg. With the bandsaw table set to a suitable angle, the cut is made, keeping the blade just clear of the disc.

This preparation work with the bandsaw saves a great deal of lathe time and the solid offcuts can yield interesting blanks for small turning.

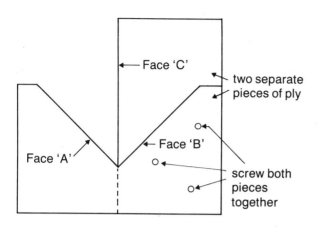

137 Centre finding jig

Finding the centre in timber which is not round can be a frustrating exercise.

I use one of three methods, depending upon the size and type of blank.

One of these methods is the ply disc which was detailed at the start of this section.

Either of the other two methods can be used on just about any size of timber depending on the size of the actual jig.

Fig. 137 shows the more complex of them. Faces 'a' and 'b' should be as near a right angle

138 Marking jig

as can be managed, and face 'c' should bisect the angle.

Faces 'a' and 'b' are held against the outer circumference of the disc, trunk or whatever, and a line is scribed along face 'c'.

The jig is now moved round by 90 degrees on the work, and the process repeated. Where the two lines cross will be the centre of the circle.

This jig can be made up in different forms and varying sizes, depending upon the type of work and degree of accuracy required.

The third of my centre-finding jigs is yet another recreation of an old idea, and yet it is bound to be new to someone.

It is simply a piece of clear perspex which has been scribed with a selection of circles – not too many, otherwise confusion sets in – and its centre is drilled out to make a tight fit for a bradawl.

The disc is offered to one face of the work and moved around until the largest continuous circle available is found, then the centre marked with the bradawl.

So much then for the three centre-finding methods which I use most often on irregularly-shaped work.

There is one more centre-finding device which I use a great deal when doing repetition work with rectangular timber. It is a block with a sharp brad in one face, the block being located in a right angle frame. (See fig. 138.)

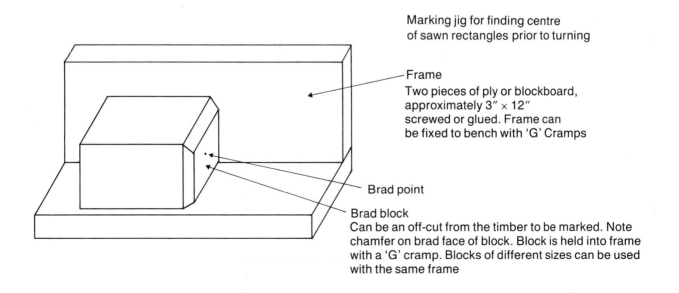

Marking jig for finding centre of sawn rectangles prior to turning

Frame
Two pieces of ply or blockboard, approximately 3" × 12" screwed or glued. Frame can be fixed to bench with 'G' Cramps

Brad point

Brad block
Can be an off-cut from the timber to be marked. Note chamfer on brad face of block. Block is held into frame with a 'G' cramp. Blocks of different sizes can be used with the same frame

The method is not ultra-accurate, but it is certainly more accurate than guessing – which I normally do!

Provided the timber is fairly consistent in size and the batch size warrants its manufacture, the jig certainly pays for itself.

The blank is placed in the jig, located on the two angled faces and then slid along so that the brad leaves its mark. The blank is now reversed with the same two faces in contact with the jig and the operation repeated. The two holes are now deepened and the work loaded on to the lathe.

The brad should not be too long, as this can lead to its becoming bent and inaccurate.

The block should also have the angled corners as shown in the sketch so that any spelch on the sawn faces doesn't stop the brad from making its mark.

17·3   Work Holding

Whilst I have already looked at the pillar drill and its use (chapter 9·5) I have made up a few work-holding jigs, some for specific jobs, but two of them for general purpose work.

The first of these is the right-angle jig which I use for repetition drilling. (See fig. 101, extreme left.) Work is located into the corner by hand.

The 'ribs' are to help avoid work being displaced by a build-up of waste from the drilling operation.

The second jig is really a cradle and is used for drilling work such as table lamps. (See fig. 103, chapter 10·5.) The gap at its base is to allow waste to fall clear of the locating faces.

Both of these jigs are held on to the table using the M6 roofing bolts, wing nuts and metal and wooden washers as detailed in chapter 9·5.

Another useful device which I have made up for repetition turning is the cradle shown in fig. 105, chapter 11·4. The sample of work can be held securely with elastic bands, if required.

The cradle should not be too close to the work to restrict access with callipers, etc.

Larger cradles or racks can be made up for heavier work.

I find it useful to have a sample of the work

not only within sight, but actually lined up with the work on the lathe, particularly on some of the more complex work I do.

Work which is to be halved after turning can be sawn using a 'vee' jig on either a circular or band saw. (See fig 139.)

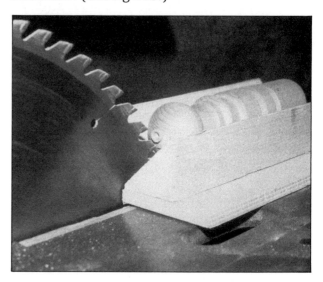

139 'Vee' jig

17·4   Racks

A couple of racks which I have made up have proved great time savers, and therefore invaluable to the repetition turner.

The first one was a combined rack for tools, callipers and pencil. (See fig. 1.) The pencil hole has a second hole drilled laterally across its base so that any extraneous shavings can be evicted.

The second rack is, in fact, more of a table in that it is principally flat. Its main advantage is that it holds articles which should be close to hand and yet out of the direct line of flight of shavings. (See fig. 140.)

The table is clamped, manacle-like, to the lathe bed, one hinged catch permitting positioning anywhere along the bed. The ubiquitous M6 bolt and wing nut permit an infinite range of adjustments to the tray in relation to the block.

The 'jollop block' is a two-position block which will support a half or near empty lacquer bottle so as to allow the brush to reach the contents. Its construction is shown in fig. 141.

140 Occasional table

141 Jollop bottle block

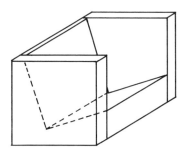

17·5 Sundries

Yet again here are a couple of ideas which I can't fit into any other category.

Firstly, a variation of the ply or hardboard discs which I have mentioned earlier in this chapter. Smaller discs are useful for marking out the sizes of table lamp bases on the self adhesive felt which is to cover the lamp base. (See fig. 142.)

142 Felt marking discs

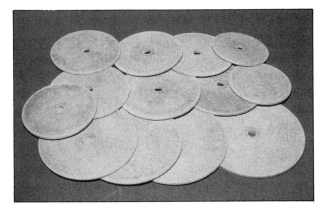

In use a disc slightly smaller than the work base diameter is positioned on the underside of the felt, which is marked and cut round carefully, the circle then being stuck in place on the work.

I prefer this method to the more commonly used one of actually marking round the base of the lamp or bowl.

Finally, I seem to collect broken foil blades like a dog collects fleas. I suppose it has something to do with being a fencing coach!

Anyway, having already described how I make up tools from the blades (chapter 9·4) I have also made up a 'table lamp pillar nipple putter in'. This device is shown in fig. 143.

The sharply-ground corners are tapped into the nipple flex hole and the nipple is then screwed into the top of the lamp.

A light blow on the underside of the handle should loosen it, leaving the nipple in place and ready to receive the lamp holder.

Should the holder not be square on the lamp, the nipple can be adjusted by re-use of the 'putter in' rather than by twisting the holder, which might tend to fracture.

A final thought on the use of pillar nipples. I like to see a slight chamfer on the top inside edge of the flex hole, rather than the insulation-cutting sharp edge, which is all too often found.

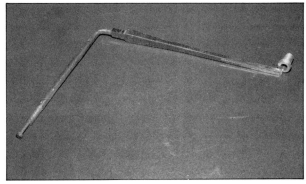

143 Table lamp pillar nipple putter in

18 Working Methods

18·1 Introduction

There are so many aspects of turning which are vital to the person who is to earn a living at the craft.

All of the preceding chapters, and most of those which follow, have their own importance. This chapter is no less important and yet it doesn't deal with any specific operations, tools etc.

18·2 'Working Methods'

This phrase covers anything which the turner does – from selecting timber for specific jobs, all the way through to chasing a customer for payment. Methods should always be looked at with an eye to improving them. The professional turner can't afford to bury his head in the sand, particularly in these days of great innovations.

The would-be serious bowl turner can't really ignore expanding chuck jaws. He should look hard at the advantages of each of these devices before rejecting their use. This may seem like a strange statement when consideration is given to the great range of expanding dovetail chucks available, but there are still a few 'bung' bowl turners about.

All turners should consider the use of high speed steel tools. I use a mixture of HSS and carbon tools, not because I reject certain HSS tools, but because I still have a long life expectancy of my carbon tools. They will eventually, no doubt, be replaced by HSS, or some other, at present secret, harder-wearing materials, when they eventually wear out.

The professional turner can't afford to ignore the methods used by others. Dismiss them after consideration by all means, but at least consider them first.

When I read some time ago that beads can be turned using a parting tool, I nearly fell out of bed laughing. Then I tried it at work the next day and immediately apologised to the writer of that particular article.

So now, I'm not too proud to look at how other turners work. My library, sparse though it is, is often raided when I have a particular problem, whether in actual tool use, or the description of that use.

And if I can't do a particular job with accepted methods, for whatever reasons, then I try new methods. The crosshand cuts in chapter 16·5, are a result of this policy. Improvise or bust, but be careful!

Even tried and tested methods can be improved upon.

For years I have made egg rings (fig. 144),

144 Egg rings

145 *Positively the fastest way to make egg rings . . . well, so far, anyway . . .·*

holding the blanks in a chuck. This meant two set-ups. The first one to prepare the timber for the chuck and the second one to actually use it.

I now do the whole operation between centres, getting a number of rings from one quick loading operation. (See fig. 145.) I also use a length of copper wire to restrain the turned rings, holding them away from the working area.

Why didn't I think of this method a few hundred rings ago?

Neither should the turner accept as gospel, the methods suggested by customers.

I am often asked to turn newel posts with a drilled hole in the top which is to accept a turned finial, also boasting a drilled hole, the two to be held together by a short length of glued dowel.

"Why not have a solid newel and finial to start with?" I ask.

Foreheads are slapped with palms of hands and phrases like "That's brilliant" are offered.

I don't tell them that my first newel posts, years ago, were in two parts, with the finial often making up the third part.

19 'Golden' Rules

19·1 Introduction

There are so many golden rules that to detail them all would take up too many pages. And even then I would miss someone's favourite, and thereby cause annoyance somewhere. And I wouldn't want to do that.

Many of these rules are no more than sound common sense. And yet, there are exceptions, depending upon the type of lathe being used, the type of work being done and, principally, the skill of the turner.

One of these rules is that the tool should always be on the tool rest before and during any cut. Sound common sense.

And yet no less an authority than the late Peter Child shows in his book a tool being used 'by hand', with the rest nowhere in sight.

Whilst I don't break that particular rule – I do not make a lot of bowls – I do give some of the rules something of a mauling. For instance:

19·2 Loading and Unloading

Chapters 9·1, 16·1 and 16·4 should be referred to here, but basically I frequently load and unload the lathe without switching it off.

This can only be done when holding the work between centres of some sort, relying on support from the tailcentre, rather than in or on a chuck. Also the work should not be too long or heavy.

Preparation is important, if not vital for this time-saving practice to be carried out safely.

First, the driving centre should be free of burrs, its point longer than its chisel edges and those edges sharp.

The work should be marked centrally with a bradawl, leaving a location hole in the work which will suit the point of the driving centre. (See fig. 82, chapter 9·1.) It will be seen that the recess will be supported somewhere on the driving centre point before the work is driven by the chisel edges. This means that the hand-held work can be loaded between driving and tailcentre points and then held lightly until the advancing tailcentre pushes the work on to the chisel edges.

After turning, the finished work is held lightly against the tailcentre with the left hand whilst the tailcentre is withdrawn slightly, allowing the work to clear itself from the chisel edges of the driving centre.

When the work stops rotating it can be grasped more firmly, removed from the lathe and the next piece placed in position.

If the work shows reluctance to leave the chisel edges, they should be checked for burrs or any other faults which might restrict the timber's withdrawal.

19·3 Working from Large Diameter to Small

'Cutting downhill' is another way of saying this, and I have had a number of watchers at craft fairs tell me that they do it, but don't know why.

It would be more accurate to say that cuts should be taken 'with the grain' where possible, but this is not easy to explain. Also, cutting downhill is not the way to work when making the bowls which come from boards.

19·4 Cutting 'Downhill'

However, let's look first of all at spindle turning. Most spindle work is done on timber which has been loaded on to the lathe with its grain running parallel to the lathe bed.

To cut with the grain therefore, any cut which is not parallel would be done from high point to low, as in the rolling pin handle shown in fig. 146.

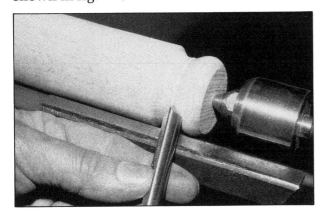

146 *With the grain*

Bert Thompson, the Canadian turner, describes this working with the grain as 'stroking the chicken'. One direction is fine, but the other direction can lead to problems. Therefore, care should taken to stop at the bottom of the cove and not allow the gouge to catch the opposite wall. Unless of course, you want the 'craggy' finish sometimes found on items offered for sale by people who should know better.

Where then, are the exceptions to the 'cutting from large diameter to small' rule? I know of, and sometimes need to use, no less than four.

147 *Against the grain*

Firstly, a light cut can be taken against the grain provided the slope up which the tool is working is not too steep (fig. 147). The final blending cut can start just inside the handle end and finish at the blade end of the bat, or even vice versa, if you are a right-handed pusher of the gouge rather than a puller.

The second exception to this rule is found when turning knotty timber. Consider a knot, such as is found in small branch wood. It runs, quite often with its friends as well, at near right angles to the growth of the main piece.

To try to cut against this usually much harder timber can cause problems, and so I usually take light cuts uphill, which means working against the rest of the grain.

Yes, I know that in an ideal world knotty timber should be avoided for turning.

The third example of the downhill cut rule getting a mauling is when the work is loaded so that the grain direction is at right angles to the lathe bed. Never done it?

Never turned plugs for cabinet makers then, have you? The cross-grained plugs are cut from the lathe produced cross grained dowel (fig. 148), fitted over sunken screws so that the

148 *Cutting 'uphill', but with the grain*

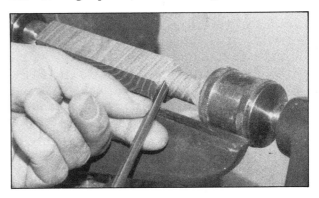

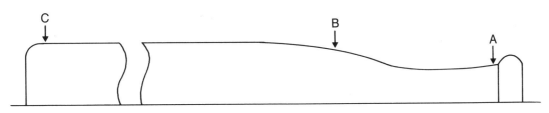

Final blending cut starts downhill at A, goes uphill at B and finishes at C

grain direction, and characteristics, match the outer surface of the work, and the plug is less noticeable than the usual filler which comes out of a tin. Anyway, the roughing cuts on such lathe work are usually done uphill with a spindle gouge.

The fourth example of uphill cuts is not quite spindle turning in that the tailcentre is not used for support as the work is held on a woodscrew chuck. (See fig. 149.)

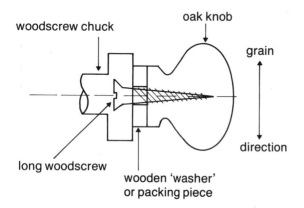

149   Woodscrew chuck

The screw is extra long on this type of work, in order to give the neck of the knob more support where it would naturally be weaker due to the grain direction.

The choice of grain direction was made by the customer, a local cabinet maker. As the timber was selected oak, some very interesting grain was exposed on the outer face of the knob.

On all of these rule benders then, the basic and easily understood principle of cutting downhill is ignored, but the harder to understand instruction to work with the grain is generally adhered to. And now you can let Bert have his chicken back!

19·5 Faceplates

Now let's look at bowls. Whilst most bowls have the grain running across them – or horizontally when the bowl is holding the family fruit – some are made with vertical grain.

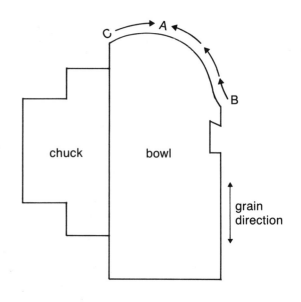

150   Working with the grain

First, the horizontal ones. Cutting downhill here is going against the grain (fig. 150). The cuts should be from 'C' to 'A' and 'B' to 'A'. When the work is reversed and hollowing starts (fig. 151) the final cuts should be made from 'E' to 'D' and 'E' to 'F'.

151   Working with the grain

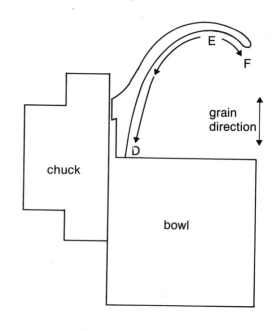

Now the vertical fruit holders (fig. 152). Here the downhill cut is back in vogue, but only on the outside cuts. 'A' to 'C' and 'A' to 'B'. The inside cuts (fig. 153) should be made from 'D' to 'E' and 'F' to 'E'.

A better shape for the vertical bowl would be as shown in fig. 154 where the grain direction does not weaken any part of the wall. All the outside cuts on this waney edge bowl were taken from rim to base, whilst the inside cuts, after gouge entry in the centre of the blank, were from base to rim.

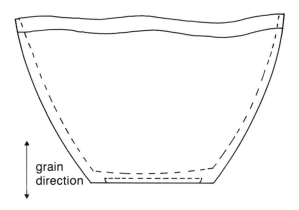

154 *Working with the grain*

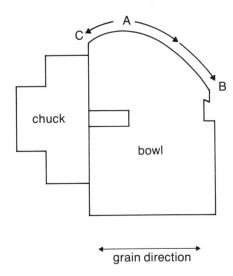

152 *Working with the grain*

153 *Working with the grain*

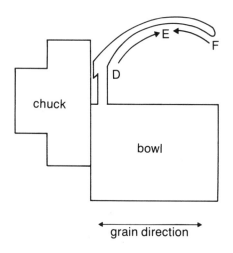

19·6 Summary

To sum up this chapter, most golden rules are based upon common sense. To ignore them is often risky, but some risks are minimised in experienced hands, and you are the best judge of when to take these risks.

When I am teaching I very rarely let my students take short cuts like using parting tool and callipers together, on the first lesson. I prefer to let confidence – both theirs and my own in them – grow first.

20 Safety

20·1 Introduction

Safety is a relative word. As I have already said in this book, certain risks are sometimes acceptable and sometimes not, depending upon the conditions.

Loading and unloading the lathe without switching it off (see chapters 16·1 and 19·2) can be done safely by experienced hands.

Rotating work can be held safely by experienced hands (chapter 16·5). If you smell pork, let go!

20·2 Common Sense

It makes sense not to remove guards from machines unless they restrict specific operations. For instance, trenching on a circular saw can't be done with the top guard in position, and so the Woodworking Machinery Regulations 1974, allow this operation to be carried out with the top guard removed.

The regulations don't however, go into anything but basic details on the use of hand lathes.

Guards should be fitted to drive belts certainly, but the rest is up to the lathe user.

If you think that what you are doing is dangerous, think hard before you do it next time.

20·3 Clothing

I like to work with my sleeves well clear of rotating parts (see cover). I also take pockets off overalls where possible to lessen the chances of the tool handle catching in them and doing naughty things at the cutting end.

Trouser pockets full of coins, keys or half-sucked toffees can cause similar problems.

I don't normally use goggles when working on the lathe, very few shavings getting much above mid-chest height, but as I now wear large lensed spectacles, the need for goggles is eliminated for most jobs.

I do wear a fairly substantial mask when working on some timbers such as iroko, afrormosia etc, or when doing a lot of sanding.

As I don't do much work in the exotic timbers I have very little experience of their effect on health, but I have suffered from sneezes, dry throats and skin irritations when using some of them.

If you experience any strange symptoms when working with new timbers, try respirators, barrier creams, an extractor point at the lathe, or even an airstream type helmet.

You do have an extractor, don't you? My first one was a vacuum cleaner.

20·4 Lighting

The stroboscopic effect can be a great problem in the workshop.

For those who don't understand this effect, it is similar to the problems of co-ordinating movie camera shutter speeds and stage coach wheel speeds which make the stage coach seem to be travelling backwards towards the pursuing Indians. For camera, substitute fluorescent striplights and for wheel spokes, substitute rotating wooden blocks.

The same effect can be found in circular saws, spindle moulders etc, and can prove to be lethal if other noisy machinery is running in the workshop, and this one seems to be stationary.

The answer is to have a localised tungsten bulb for each machine. Certainly my lathes have their own lamp, which is adjustable so as to cast a shadow where I want it. I also like to wear a peaked cap when working, so as to keep the light out of my eyes should the lamp have to be positioned at a difficult height.

20·5   Factory Inspectorate

I have defended 'the enemy' on a number of occasions. The enemy here being the dreaded factory inspector.

The regulations which the inspector has to interpret cannot be specific on all subjects in every detail. If they were, they would need an edifice the size of the British Museum to house them, and an infinity of articled clerks to keep them up to date.

Interpretation must be done on site by the inspector and the workshop or factory occupant.

My own experience of the inspectors is that once they realise I am not trying to hide anything from them, they remain firm but also fair. But maybe I have been lucky so far.

It is our fingers they are trying to protect, so why fight them?

20·6   Conclusion

When it comes to the crunch – if that is not an unfortunate choice of word – it is down to the common sense of the machine operator to avoid accidents.

I used to say to my employees, ''These machines don't know the difference between beech and bone, so they will chobble their way through anything which you care to feed into them''.

21 General Maintenance

21·1 Introduction

I am not talking here of clear floors, clean windows, dust-free overhead fittings, etc. Those things should be automatic anyway, especially where woodturning machinery is concerned.

The following are a collection of little more than handy hints, not always obvious, until you read them, that is.

21·2 Lubrication

I use a generally available lubricating oil – 20/50 motor oil – in plastic detergent bottles for most of my workshop lubrication, unless of course the machinery manufacturers have specified something different.

If a particular set of machine bearings seems to be full of gunge – or for the more pedantic amongst you, an accumulation of lubricating oil, dust, shavings and other debris – then I usually clean the bearing by running a light oil through it until the oil comes out clear, and then start over again with the 20/50 oil. If that doesn't do the trick, then strip down and clean thoroughly. Then do the same with the bearing.

Some of the proprietary brands of workshop maintenance lubricants are most useful not only in restoring shiny metal surfaces which have become tarnished, but also in removing the build up of resin etc., which clogs saw blades, turning tools and anything else it comes into contact with, when some types of timber are being worked.

21·3 Rust Repellent

I like to keep a few dry shavings about in any boxes or trays containing tools. The idea is that the shavings will attract any moisture which might otherwise find a more permanent home in the surface of the metal. These shavings need to be changed periodically of course, otherwise they will become counter productive by holding the moisture against the tools which they should be protecting.

21·4 Brushes

A paperhanger's brush of 6″ or more is useful for lathe and bench cleaning etc., as the bristles are more resilient than some softer brushes.

I also like to keep a natural bristle brush close to hand, and this I use to clear the shavings or sanding dust from the inside crevices of a bowl prior to finishing the bowl. (See fig. 155.)

I differentiate between the two types of brush so that I reduce the risk of rubbing headstock lubricating oil into the important little places of the bowls by using the wrong brush.

21·5 Metal Working

Although I have a selection of woodturning lathes in the workshop, I find my old, almost worn-out engineering lathe very useful for repairing or modifying drive centres, holding devices or whatever.

saw complete the machinery maintenance department.

Before I had my engineering lathe, I made friends with a tame engineer who needed odd woodturning jobs done from time to time. We bartered.

155 *Natural and synthetic bristles*

The lathe has facilities for thread cutting, although they are not complete. If I need some device with a thread on it, I usually buy a nut or bolt with the appropriate thread and machine the body to suit.

An engineering vice, a collection of files, hand tools, the usual taps and dies and a hack-

22 Professional Insights

22·1 Introduction

This chapter contains information which will probably be new to many readers and therefore of use to most of them.

Whilst it is almost the last chapter which deals with the technique of cutting wood, it is most certainly not the end of the important section of the book. Not for the would-be professional anyway.

There is a lot more to being a professional turner than just turning professionally.

One of the questions which I needed an answer to way back in 1969 was whether I would still enjoy turning when doing it full time. I was the only person who could answer such a question and only then in the light of experience.

The answer is that I do still enjoy it, but I also enjoy the breaks from actual production lathe work which I get when doing my administration, writing, teaching etc.

I also wondered just how many turners earned a living solely from the produce of their own lathe and how many had to augment their income by selling to other lathe users.

I suspect the answer to that question will never be found, but I am confident that most of the professional turners, of whatever grade, find an extra income from writing, teaching, selling hardware etc., of great use. I know I do.

One of the frustrations which I soon found with turning was that I rarely saw the finished item *in situ*. Usually the last I see of my work is when it goes out of the workshop door.

22·2 Work Methods

Some people are gregarious, needing people about them for stimulation, companionship etc., whilst others are reclusive, preferring their own company for much of the time. The professional woodturner needs to be a little bit of each.

With too many distractions around, reasonable work rates cannot be kept up, but without the stimulation of others, it is all too easy to suffer from a lowering of quality.

My answer to this continual problem is to visit other turners when I can, be stimulated by them and what they are doing, and then to lock myself away and work, hopefully refreshed.

I don't do my visits during their production time, of course, but talk with them during craft fairs, seminars etc.

When working, I try not to turn with a closed mind, or to use my own methods to the exclusion of all others. I am prepared to try someone else's sytem, or modifications of my own which occur to me from time to time. These are the things which keep me sane despite being an isolationist.

I have, in the past, received some help from CoSIRA, although not so much with lathework as with router jig making and costing new jobs.

CoSIRA, The Council for Small Industries in Rural Area, offers workshop visits, courses and many other services which the newly self-employed entrepreneur would find of interest. The nearest office can be found in the local telephone directory.

22·3 Do's

Here are some time-saving ideas.

I am a great list maker. I have a series of clipboards about the workshop, each one with its own title, on which I write the important things, as they are 'thunked', which I need to do before they escape again from my sieve-like memory. I used to write on lumps of wood and put them in my back pocket so that their presence would be felt when I sat down, but I no longer have unlimited access to suitable pieces of ply. I *do* still have the scars though.

When sawing blanks for production work, any offcuts which I get are usually sawn into smaller standard sizes straight away.

I find it easier to stack blanks for garden dibbers, needle cases or what have you, on a shelf than to store sundry longer lengths of timber offcuts about the workshop where they are going to get forgotten, fallen over and cursed.

Small lengths of timber left in the lathe chuck can be turned into a dolls' house plate, small candlestick or whatever, rather than merely removed from the chuck and thrown away.

I have found that a captive nut (see fig. 156) is sometimes easier to use than a wing nut in certain applications. I use the system to secure my demonstration lathe to its portable bench. Provided the block is large enough, sufficient torque can be obtained and no time lost in searching for spanners at packing up time.

156 Captive nut assembly

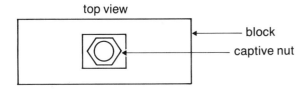

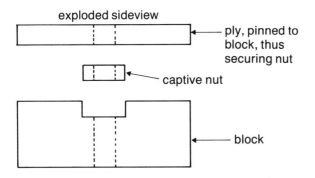

I have seen lots of turners working on lathes which have not had thread protectors fitted to the headstock spindle.

Whilst I agree that any turner who frequently runs his tool into the thread does not deserve the title of turner, I do like to have the thread protector fitted wherever possible as it helps in the removal of taper fitting driving centres etc., which occasionally become tight in the spindle. Any armourers amongst you may remember the principle of primary extraction, which is the initial loosening of a taper in its bore, prior to withdrawal.

Incidentally, if such a centre is tight, both it and the bore of the spindle should be checked for damage after removal, and then the damage rectified so as to avoid a recurrence of the condition.

22·4   Don'ts

Here are some additions to the almost endless list of things not to do. Well, rarely to *do*, anyway.

First of all, an obvious one which also comes under the heading of safety.

Don't ever wrap any finishing device round your finger before applying it to the rotating work. Particular care should be taken when using steel wool or a polishing cloth which still has loose strands on it.

I think E.T. was a woodturner. In fact when I think if his finger lighting up at the end, I *know* he was a woodturner.

When doing work which boasts sharp corners, watch out for your knuckles. Chair and table legs are bad enough, the square sections of such work having claimed a meter or two of my outer layer over the years. But these waney edged bowls can be most disturbing, especially when the inner surface is being sanded. I deliberately use small pieces of sandpaper on such work, so that I can be sure about the whereabouts of all of it, thus allowing me to concentrate on knuckle clearance. But still they get me!

When applying the lacquer to lathe work, I usually have the work stationary – but not always. If, for instance, I am making eggs in public, I often leave the lathe running for all of the finishing operation, including lacquering.

I do shield the public from the spray, of course.

My reason for this application during rotation is to achieve that visual impact on the watchers when the egg finally comes to rest in my hand, exposing the grain to the viewing audience.

What they saw loaded into the chuck as a rather ordinary piece of wood suddenly becomes a beautifully marked egg. That way I sell more eggs that I would if they saw the stationary egg being lacquered.

I also apply lacquer to small items whilst the lathe is running, there being little chance of missing any areas on such stuff.

A lot of my work is in replacing worn out or broken parts for furniture restorers and the like.

Quite often the part to be replaced has suffered the ravages of the dreaded woodworm and whenever such timber is brought into the workshop I cocoon it in polythene as a precaution against the little beasties colonizing any of my own timber.

22·5 Copying

'Imitation is the sincerest form of flattery', a true statement maybe, but it is of small comfort if you are the one being flattered by someone else who is also undercutting you.

There will always be the occasions where copying someone else's work is actually desirable. Making replacement parts for furniture is only one such. There will also be occasions when it is advantageous to work for a minimum profit, or even for no profit at all. I have sometimes done 'lost leaders', or work which I have lost on, in order to gain a larger order from the same customer. See chapter 23·2 on costing.

However, to regularly copy others is the easy way out. Better to develop your own style. Be inspired by the work of others but improve on their ideas, or better still, develop your own. That way you will become an established turner and also push the craft into new and unexplored areas of development.

22·6 Trade Associations

There are benefits to be gained from joining some of the trade associations. For instance, I pay a regular registration fee to a society which, in return, will chase bad debtors, conduct discreet credit worthiness enquiries into new customers, and carry out other similar functions at low rates. On the bad debt side they have succeeded where other, more expensive organizations, have failed.

To join an association which is more involved with promoting craftsmanship generally, or a specific craft in particular, is a decision which only the individual can make.

If you feel that you need acceptance by your peers, an emblem which is recognised by the public either nationally or locally, or the backing of an organization which will support and guide you, then ask around. There will almost certainly be some member near you whose opinion you would value. An annual membership fee is a form of insurance. You pay the premium, hoping never to have to make a claim against the policy. Provided the premium is not too high, then membership can be a good idea.

23 Administration and Costing

23·1 Introduction

Administration is a necessary evil. All paperwork and no production work will lead to an exercise demanded of you by the bank manager, to assess why you have made no profit. All production work and no record of purchases, costs, sales, etc., will lead to the same demand from the same source and for the same reason.

But before we get bogged down in the paperwork, let's make some basic decisions. Whilst there is usually a good market for well made items which the public wants, or can be made to realise it wants, the price has to be right. Chapter 23·2 on costing deals with this important aspect.

I do very little selling of household goods through shops, most of this type of work being sold direct.

I also do a lot of industrial work, when it is needed. Whilst I can't compete with the automatic machines which produce turnings very quickly, I can still win out over them on some jobs where the batch sizes remain too small to warrant setting the machine, where the work does not lend itself to such machines or where the machine is full for some weeks and I can do a quicker turn round of the work, if you will excuse the pun.

The decision then is what kind of work to do, and how to sell it?

Having a foot in both the household and commercial camps as I do can lead to problems when both areas of the trade are busy. I can't afford to say "No" to either type of work when it comes along.

My solution is to build up stocks of what I know the public will buy, during the quiet times, and to do the industrial turning when the orders come in.

If many orders are coming in then practical delivery dates need to be agreed, and kept. A calendar type progress board will help here. (See fig. 157.) If not much work is coming in then just a piece of paper on a notice board giving details of the order would suffice. Keep it simple. Incidentally, an old fridge door and some small magnets make the ideal noticeboard. It's easy to maintain as well!

When I first became involved with administration in a factory, rather than the shop floor practical work which I had been used to, I was given a piece of excellent advice. My new boss, the production controller said "Reg, you have to have a system. If it doesn't work, you can alter it so that it does. But with no system, when something goes wrong, you can't do a thing to avoid the problem next time round." My daily system is dealt with in chapter 23·3.

23·2 Costing

There are many ways to cost a job. When, way back in 1969, I set out to conquer the world armed only with a lathe, a broom and a kettle, I decided to be sneaky.

I was asked to quote on saucepan lid knobs from teak, in batches of 500, per month. I contacted a well established company who produced this type of thing, got a price from them and knocked a few per cent off it.

When I quoted my price to the potential customer, he laughed his socks off.

I ended up doing the work for about ⅓rd of the quoted price and still made a reasonable profit, once I had my methods sorted out.

The larger company which I had approached probably had a dozen or so enquiries each week from those such as myself, knew that I was trying it on and their reply taught me

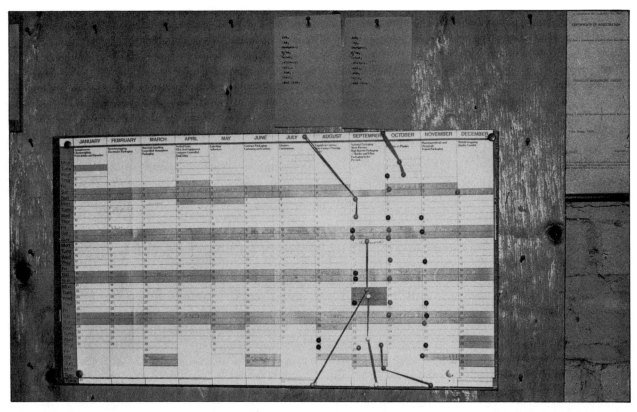

157 *Lead time board*

a valuable lesson. Work out your own prices and stand on your own feet. You'll soon know if you got it wrong.

So how then, do I arrive at a basic price for a product? The first thing I need to know is how much it will cost me to produce. The following figures are simplified for convenience, but should be as accurate as possible when you do your costing exercise.

Outgoings (workshop running costs)

	£
Annual rent	1,500
Annual rates	300
Insurance (building, contents, work in hand, public liability etc.)	250
Power	150
Travel costs (car, petrol, oil etc.)	500
Postage, advertising, stationery	300
Phone	200
Repairs to machines etc.	100
Consumables (screws, glue etc.)	100
Tools	50
	3,450
Own wages	10,000
Total	£13,450

I have put wages last in the order of outgoings, and this is quite deliberate. All the other expenditures HAVE to be met and anything left over goes towards wages, unless of course you are going to employ, in which case employees wages etc., find their place on the MUST list, whilst your own are placed even more firmly on the 'anything left?' list.

This total cost is then:

Divided by 48 working weeks = £280·20/week
Divided by 5 working days/week = £56·04/day
Divided by 6 actual working hours/day = £9·34/hour

So, being self-employed means I have to find more than £9 an hour. Divide the hourly sum into 60 minutes and you will see why I don't like to stop for even a minute, unless I have to.

This costing formula is part firm figures – rent, rates etc. – and part estimated. If in doubt ask an accountant. (See chapter 23·7.)

So, having established the annual, weekly, daily, hourly and even minute by minute running costs, ask yourself if you still want to be self-employed. If the answer is still yes, then ask amongst your friends to see if anyone can recommend a good psychiatrist. But whilst you are waiting for an appointment, do an exercise to arrive at a selling price on something which you have recently made.

You must of course, know how long it took you to make. And that is not just lathe time. Was the blank not selected, sawn, marked for centre and loaded on to the lathe before the green button was pressed? And neither does the timing stop when you press the red button on the lathe. You still have to remove the finished work, inspect it, pack it and store it. All of these operations take time, as does tool sharpening, lathe setting, calliper setting and a few other forgotten, but equally important, jobs.

In fact, I consider tool sharpening to be part of the six hours' actual working time which is covered in my original costing formula.

Lathe and calliper setting, making ready abrasive paper, lacquer, wax etc., I consider to be non-productive work, which must be done outside those six daily hours.

Again, for the ease of simplification, let's consider that we are to cost the making of a rolling pin.

We estimate that all the preparation work has been done in 1 minute.

The lathe work, 'load' to 'unload', or fixing to removing is completed in three minutes. Inspecting, packing etc. takes one minute (OK I said I was simplifying the exercise).

This gives us the formula £9·34/hour, divided by 60 minutes, multiplied by 5 minutes for each item, or $\frac{£9·34}{6} \times 5 = ·778$, say 78p each. That has found the labour cost.

Now for the timber cost. As you will have realised by now, I'm all for the simple life when it comes to maths. And so, our rolling pin is made from a 12″ length of 2″ square timber. And the timber cost me £20 per cubic foot, inclusive of whatever tax is prevalent at the time. One cubic foot contains 1,728 cubic inches. So we get the formula:

$$\frac{£20·00 \times 2″ \times 2″ \times 12″}{1728} = £0·555$$

But this timber cost makes no allowance for waste. Most timber merchants measure from one end of a board to the other, regardless of end splits, knots etc., and charge accordingly. And so do I.

I usually add beteween 10% and 25% to my timber cost, depending upon timber condition, possible further use by me of offcuts, colour of customer's eyes, etc. Let's in this case allow for a 10% scrap allowance. This takes the timber cost up to 61p.

So now we have:

Labour	78p)	
Timber	61p)	Total cost £1·39p.

Finished?
No way!!!
We need a profit. If we don't aim to make a profit, we will be standing still. This profit needs to be used either to buy new, or at least repair existing machinery. And not just in the workshop. Is the typewriter, computer, car or whatever, not falling to pieces?

My usual profit margin is 20%, but this varies from job to job, depending upon batch size, potential of further business from the same customer, how quickly he will pay, and whatever.

So:

Cost price	£1·39
Profit @ 20%	£0·28
Selling price	£1·67

So now you go and tell Auntie Alice that the 50 pence she just paid you for her brand new, lathe-fresh rolling pin, was only a down payment and you'll be round later for the balance.

That is basically the formula which I use. I gain when I can do the job in less time than I have costed it at, without losing out on quality.

I also gain when I can use offcuts for which I have already made an allowance and therefore have been paid for, on another job, thus charging for them again. I gain when I have found a better source of supply for the timber.

I can just as easily lose out on any of these points – the work taking longer than I had allowed for, the timber, having been sawn by me being found to be faulty but non-returnable, or the source of cheaper timber having dried up (he went broke because he was too cheap!)

I keep a record of all my costings, times etc. as I often find that some parts of new jobs are identical to existing work, which gives me a more accurate idea of the time involved.

I actually time myself on repetition work, using a stop watch and a clipboard. Depending upon how long each item takes, I time them individually, in batches of 10 or even of 50 or more, through one particular operation.

I do sometimes put a much higher profit than the 10% to 25% figure on to some work. For instance, if I get a rush job which means that I must put in some extra time at work to get the customer out of trouble, then I apply my 'fire engine' profit of 50% or so. In fact one of my customers now refers to me as 'the fireman'.

23·3 Daily Administration

Let's assume that I get a new enquiry from someone and it is worthwhile my doing a costing exercise on it – and not all of my enquiries would get this far!

I record the customer and job details on a costing sheet, together with the date. I then work out a price, inform the customer and file the sheet under the customer's name.

Let us now assume that the customer says ''Yes, please'', which does sometimes happen. We agree a completion date which is practical and I record the starting date and completion date on my progress chart (fig. 157, chapter 23·1), together with the customer's name and the enquiry date. I order the timber, should it not be from my own stock, to be delivered in time for the starting date.

When the time comes to start the work, I make up any pin sticks etc., that will be needed, giving them the same enquiry date for future reference. I note their existence on the cost sheet, or the process specification if the job is complicated, and when the work is completed I hang the sticks up on a rail, in their dated order (fig. 158) for future use.

When the job is finished, I make out an invoice by hand, using a standard duplicate invoice book. If the batch isn't completed before the customer starts taking delivery then I record the part batches in a packing note book – simply an untitled but numbered duplicate

158 *Pin sticks*

book – get a signature for the goods and complete the invoice, quoting packing note numbers and quantities, when the whole order is finished.

Depending upon the customer, I sometimes simply submit the original handwritten invoice, with my stamp, label or whatever at its head – so that they know where to send the cheques – or I type out the invoice on a letterhead. This takes more time, but it looks better.

If you are registered for Value Added Tax, then you must retain a duplicate of the submitted invoice for inspection purposes.

Sales which I make at craft fairs etc., are recorded on a 'monthly sales' invoice, which is merely the next available invoice in the book at the start of each month.

When invoices are paid I record the method – cash or cheque – and the date and, if cheques or large sums of cash are concerned, I record the invoice number and the amount on the paying-in slip at the bank.

Cash payments in small sums go straight into my petty cash ledger.

The duplicate copies of paid invoices are folded in half in the invoice book. In this way I can tell at a glance what invoices are outstanding at any one time.

This system of day-to-day recording may sound complex, but I can assure you that it is not as complex as some which I have seen.

Workshop time is precious to me and must be spent working with wood, not paper.

When I need to make purchases, I rarely use purchase orders. A note of what I have ordered, from whom and when is usually sufficient, and this can be pinned to the 'shopping list' board in the workshop.

Should the supplier require an official order number then my initials and the date is usually sufficient for him.

Once again, this is the easy way, but why make problems? I should be able to remember that I have requested 50 feet of 6″ × 2″ beech without making a lot of paperwork out of it. I also tend to order account items such as timber at the start of the month so as to gain some extra working time before the bills have to be met.

The other two books which I use – but not daily – are ledgers.

First comes the main ledger, which shows income from sales (taken from records in the bank paying-in book) and large purchases or other cheque book transactions, taken from cheque book stubs.

The second ledger is for petty cash.

Any income from small sales which are paid in cash are recorded in this book, and so are purchases such as odd tools, petrol, coffee, work boots and so on. Receipts should be obtained for all such purchases, of course.

I don't use a petty cash tin, as most businesses do. Any transactions go into or out of the money I have with me at that moment. In this way, it is possible on occasion to have a minus figure in petty cash, a fact that drove one poor young tax inspector to distraction when he paid me a routine visit some time ago.

As most of my work is for specific orders and no two customers want the same style of table legs, wooden knobs etc, stock control of finished items is no great problem. However, I do have such a system for the craft items.

Making such things as rolling pins, table lamps, bowls or whatever, in economical batches, makes sense financially for the timber purchasing and also from the point of view of setting up. Storage can however, be another matter.

If we were travelling to a craft fair my wife used to complain about having too many boxes full of things which we wouldn't sell, whilst I tended to favour the 'if we haven't brought it with us we can't sell it' theory.

Now I have a permament workshop where stocks can be held and when the levels get below their individually set limits, another batch is produced.

We still have the arguments on 'how much of what to take to where?' when we travel, but my wife now rarely runs out of anything, and when she does she keeps quiet in case I start crowing.

One last, but most important point on this subject of records. Prices of steady selling items should reviewed periodically.

The craft work is costed en-masse each January, allowances made for probable increases in costs – principally timber – and the new selling price fixed for the year. Other work is costed as the orders arrive.

It is very easy to lose sight of the fact that your purchase costs are continually creeping up whilst your selling prices tend to be static.

23·4 New Customers

When I get an enquiry from a new customer, I like to know a number of things: If the items requested have been made before, why have they suddenly come to me? Whilst there are many genuine reasons to look for a new supplier it might just be that credit has run out with the old one.

If the request is for a new product then I like to know what the ultimate use is to be, so as to offer a better service.

For instance, I once had an enquiry for 1¾″ diameter wooden balls in lots of 200. After a couple of questions, I found out that they were to be drilled, dowelled and mounted on to the tops of 1¾″ square wooden posts which were also to be drilled to take the dowel.

I suggested that the balls could be turned from the solid but slightly longer posts, thus saving an expensive assembly operation. I got the order and a lot more orders to follow.

However, some customers are wary of giving too much information to a stranger, so don't over-pry or you might lose a sale.

If I have any suspicion of a problem with payment from the new customer, I ask for trading terms which will cut down my risk. The ultimate answer is to submit a pro forma invoice, which means that the goods must be paid for on receipt of the invoice and before they are despatched – or even made, in extreme cases.

There are variations on this theme. For instance, 'half the payment with order to cover the cost of timber, the balance on completion of the work' or 'the balance after 30 days', or whatever you are prepared to risk. A discount for prompt payment can be another incentive to a customer new or old.

A well-known turner – a canny lad from the north east of England – once told me about a contract which he had for a lot of balusters. The customer was well-known locally for not paying on time. The deal was struck, payment on delivery of goods. The goods were delivered, payment was not made – he had left his cheque book at home – and so our canny lad said "You are ten short of your required number and so the job, and all the sub-contractors will be held up until I have been paid. The ten are in my workshop". He was paid the same day. Nice one, Allan.

When I do a new job for someone I don't keep samples of the work. In fact, if I had done so I would have had a workshop full of samples by now, with no space for either me or the lathe. However, I do often photograph specials, so as to have something to discuss with potential customers who may be looking for similar work.

23·5 Advertising

I have, on odd occasions, taken out advertisements in the local press if work seems to be drying up, but I have never needed to spend a lot of money on such advertisements.

Usually the word 'woodturning' in bold type catches the eye of potential customers. I feel that the British Telecom directory has brought in as much work as any form of advertising, and that entry is part of the cost of hiring the phone in the first place. And neither do I spend extra on a bold type entry as I am the only woodturner on this exchange.

Of course, any special services which go beyond mere production, should be advertised in appropriate journals. For instance, I advertise the fact that I run courses of instruction, that I am a demonstrator and that I give talks on turning.

All of these aspects of my work are advertised in woodworking magazines.

The demonstration service is mentioned on my literature which goes out to other people within the trade, and the 'talks' facility is very much in evidence at craft fairs which I attend or for members of the public who visit my workshop on open days.

23·6 Time Wasting

Whilst on the subject of workshop visitors, it is very easy to fall into the habit of having a chat with callers.

I chat, but I work whilst I am doing it. If the caller is merely passing the time of day then he is probably a regular visitor and will soon learn that he has to talk whilst I work.

If he is selling something then I give him five minutes and then if I am not in the market to buy, either I start the lathe and cover him in shavings, or I sell him something, having steered the conversation in that direction.

One of my early woodturning students made a time-glass as a project. He keeps it on his office desk and whenever a visitor walks in to see him he turns it over. "What's that?" they can't avoid asking. "It's a four-minute timer" he says. "When the sand runs out, so do you!"

I also try to stop members of the public from getting into the workshop except on open days, even if they want to purchase something which I have made. They usually want to see *all* the table lamps, bowls or whatever, and I can lose twenty minutes per sale, which means that I should be charging an extra £3·00 on top of the normal selling price. The time for such sales is on open days, when I have someone manning the sales table and who is probably working on a commission basis.

All this may sound very harsh, but so is life for the self-employed person.

I have a notice in my workshop window which says that whilst I don't mind being watched through the glass, I can't afford to stop for a chat. The workshop will next be open on such and such a date and in the meantime, samples of my work can be purchased at the following places . . .

Customers often bring me work which would be described as 'Saturday jobs'. That is, jobs which can be done on Saturday, when the boss isn't about.

Whilst I don't have Saturday jobs as such, I do have a list of odd jobs which can be fitted into the regular programme.

I may, for instance, be waiting for a delivery of timber, final instructions on a production job, or whatever. It may even be that a job was finished ahead of time.

I like to have a few odd jobs about which can be done as time fillers for such moments. I have even used them as teaching projects in the past. It may have worked out that they were completed on Saturday, but it was just as likely to have been somewhere between Sunday and Friday.

23·7 Administration Specialists

I still group administration under the same

heading as the weekly visit to the supermarket – a necessary evil.

And I have the same policy regarding them both. My wife can save a lot of money on the weekly 'supermarket grand prix' by knowing more about the subject than I do.

Likewise, an accountant can save you more money than he charges in fees by knowing what to claim allowances for, what the legal jargon on official forms actually means in everyday English and how to produce a yearly balance sheet for bank managers, income tax inspectors, or whoever.

I am well represented in both areas, that is, matrimony and accountancy. In matrimony, I first met my wife when she was but two years old and I was ahead of her in worldly experience by a full four years.

In accountancy, I asked around and got a short list of names to avoid. Needless to say, I didn't ask the accountants. Nobody cries "stinking fish for sale". I asked fellow small business people like myself.

I have, from time to time, had recourse to use other specialists, one notable occasion being when a landlord was wanting to increase the next three years' rent by what I considered an unacceptable figure. The independent rent assessor whom I employed got the increase halved and charged me just less than he had saved me in the first year.

24 Craft Fairs and Demonstrations

24·1 Introduction

A lot of turners are not able to work in public for a variety of reasons. Maybe they don't have suitably light lathes or benches which can be transported; they don't make the type of products which lend themselves to public demonstrations; they don't like being watched.

There are lots of reasons for shunning public stare. There are also lots of reasons for attracting it.

If I have an audience, I can usually get some chat going with them, increasing the crowds round the lathe, which is a natural crowd puller anyway. And if I have the people watching, I should be able to sell them something.

Of course, once anyone stands up in front of a crowd, he is there to be shot at. That is an occupational hazard.

24·2 Venues

My wife, daughters and I have suffered many excruciating experiences at venues ranging from 4 star hotels with plush carpet, down to open air and muddy feet.

My decision to start attending craft fairs was forced upon me when the industrial turning, which I had been concentrating on, at last dried up due to the recession of the late 70s and early 80s.

I soon found out that some venues cost a lot of money and didn't repay it with sales, whereas other venues cost little but had a good return.

When I did regular fairs, I usually took the lathe with me, to attract more people to the event.

I usually got the lathe space for nothing, the event organizers realising that live demonstrations which could be advertised were a great incentive to public attendance.

Some organizers are better than others at getting the public through the door. Only experience will tell you who to avoid, but I soon learned to avoid organizations which didn't limit the numbers of any particular craft. I have been one of four turners at a fair with as few as twenty crafts people.

Now, happily, I am in the situation where the public usually come to me, although I do venture out from time to time, having a few regular venues which I know from past experience are good ones.

I was once offered a week at a flower festival, as one of ten crafts people, each of us in an individual unit of some 100 sq. ft. The units were situated in a large city park, to which thousands of people flocked during the week.

It was a failure. The problem was that people simply wouldn't put their feet over the threshold. They were outside, in an open space and there was a psychological barrier at the doorway of the unit which very few people managed to overcome. And this despite the attraction of the lathe.

However, some venues which seem to be a dead loss at the time, do turn out well in the end.

For instance, I have had enquiries for lathes, lessons and long production runs after being seen, and heard, at what seemed at first to be losing days . . . So you can never be absolutely sure.

24·3 Format

Having decided to try the craft fair circuit, I had to decide what to make.

I kept it simple, as the greater the variety of work I was to undertake, the greater would be the amount of hardware I would have to carry.

I avoided bowls and other large face plate work as I didn't want to cover the clients with shavings and dust.

Spindle and small screwchuck work then, meant that most of the shavings would stay on my side of the lathe.

I also decided to work behind a perspex guard, for three reasons. Firstly, it keeps most of the little fingers out of the shavings and tools on the bench. Secondly, it retains most of the few shavings which do go forward from the lathe rather than behind it.

Thirdly, it stops tools from falling forward into the crowd. It is surprising how soon a tool will lost its edge when it comes into contact with bone!

I also decided to employ a sales person to man the stand whilst I worked on the lathe. A lot of what I made was deliberately aimed at pocket money and was therefore placed on the front of the sales table.

I couldn't keep my eye on it and work safely as well.

My wife and daughters soon came to recognise the different timbers and also picked up a lot of the technicalities from listening to my chat.

24·4 Display

We found, by trial and error, that the way goods are displayed has a lot to do with how well they sell.

OK, that is fairly obvious, but it is still worth considering different layouts from time to time.

One particular line which I have been making for some years was simply not noticed by a regular customer, until it was displayed on a felt covered box and therefore raised up from its normal position on the table.

24·5 Repartee (OK – Chat!)

Getting the customers laughing is, I have found, a useful advantage sometimes, but it shouldn't be overdone.

The main object of demonstrating is to sell. In my case, I am selling either goods or courses.

If I get a technical question and have time to answer it in depth, I will do, as that could quite well lead to recruiting another student.

If I have a crowd who are not responsive and who are not buying either, then I stop work for a while, announcing the fact that I have to sharpen the tools, go for a break, or whatever. I have even been known to try rudeness.

''Shall we all join hands and try to contact the living?''

But I make sure there aren't any heavies in the crowd first!

I have found, on occasion, that if a particular product isn't selling too well and I start making them on the lathe, then sales increase.

I also make a point of doing jobs which take no more than ten minutes each, as people like to see a finished article, usually even wanting to buy 'the one that has just been made'.

It is also of benefit to make a few of each item, once the lathe is set up for that particular job.

People don't want to see callipers being set or tool rests being adjusted, they want shavings and changing shapes.

Also, when they get fed up with watching the tenth whatever it is, they will move on and give someone else a chance to watch.

24·6 Educating

One advantage of being able to talk to the public about what I make is the fact that I can do some educating.

A few days ago I was making a number of wine bottle stoppers from pine, a couple of which were knotty. A lady said that the knotty ones should be reduced in price.

I talked about the extra beauty of the grain, the shape of the stopper being dictated by the position of the knot and the problems in turning such timber due to change in grain direction, texture etc.

I don't know whether I convinced her in the end, but some of the listeners nodded in agreement with me when I suggested that the price should be increased rather than decreased.

24·7 Innovations

Beauty is indeed in the eye of the beholder.

I have been responsible for some creations which just would not go right, were put on the sales table to get reactions from the public and were promptly sold.

Other things which I have made, enjoyed, and been reluctant to sell have experienced a second reluctance, this time from the puchaser.

Whilst I often feel that I want to do the kind of work which I really enjoy, I also know that I must eat.

To make things which the public are not yet ready to buy is a good way to fail as a businessman.

I tend to make things which I know will sell. Although I could easily become bored with them, I put up with it for a few days, in order to gain enough time to indulge myself by making things which really interest me, but which are slow sellers.

Of course, were I of independent means, I could make what I wanted, fill the shelves and simply wait for the occasional purchaser amongst all the other sneerers.

It is no good just making translucent bowls if the people you are selling to are looking for Cox's Orange Pippin containers.

Likewise, I tend to make something like one spalted beech bowl for seven 'ordinary' ones because I know that is just about right for the present buying trends.

Be innovative, but unless you have another source of income, keep some of the dull, boring, good sellers on the stand as well.

And speaking of innovations, be inspired by other turners' work. Don't copy, improve. I know that I have offered this advice before, but it is well worth a second mention. Discuss your work with others and listen to what they say.

The nice thing about advice is that you don't have to take it, but if enough people make the same comments, maybe they are right.

Don't ever stop learning.

24·8 Preparation

When I did my first public demonstration I only had two Coronet Major lathes, with standard length beds.

The Major was not built with easy transportation in mind and it took four journeys to get everything on site.

I was working in a marquee which had been pitched in a wet field.

As the day progressed the headstock end of the lathe table sank lower and lower and I ended up working something like 20 degrees out of the horizontal.

It was shortly after that experience I bought the Minor lathe. Much lighter! Mind you, it took me a further four years to think of putting it on wheels.

I also, as I have already said, travel light, although a first aid kit for lathes is a good idea. things like spare fuses, Allen keys etc., have a permanent home in the travelling tray.

I have also marked everything that travels with me with a band of yellow paint. that way I can have a quick look round the workshop after I have packed for a fair, and anything sporting a yellow stripe gets thrown into the trailer as well.

And, of course, anyone who works in public, who teaches, or allows non-employees into the workshop, should be insured.

You all are, of course?

25 Employment

25·1 Introduction

To employ or not to employ, that is the question. Once again, sorry Will.

Having been an employer for a few years, four or five in total, I can honestly say I did not enjoy the experience.

I spent too much time on administration, watching out for expensive clangers and trying to keep up production schedules. My interest and excitement comes from doing rather than organizing.

Happily, however, not all people are the same. Some of you may be potential employers.

25·2 Choices

The decision to look for extra help is usually forced upon the small manufacturer when he suddenly gets a large order, a deadline is brought forward or he – for some other reason – can't cope.

The choices he has to make are a) work longer hours, b) employ, c) use subcontractors.

In the short term, option a) is probably the best solution. I have put in many sixty-hour weeks in order to complete work on time. Of course, the strain tells after a while, not only on the worker but also on the family.

Option b) is what most people would go for . . . Dreams of the work being done by minions whilst you sit back digesting business lunches. Well, it happens on the telly, but it never happened to me.

In fact, most one man shows which suddenly start to employ usually decide to work alongside the employees.

This means that the burden of extra administration – wages, tax returns, holiday rotas etc., has to be done either at night, or by someone else, who must also be paid but is not doing direct labour. That is, not making something which can be sold to pay the wages.

My own preference now would be for option c).

I have taught a number of local hobby turners who could subsequently come into my workshop, and work for themselves using my lathes, on a piecework basis.

I have used this system in the past, getting the turner to invoice me at the end of each batch, week's work or whatever, and paying on receipt of that invoice.

They are working on a self-employed basis, declare their own earnings and keep my administration problems down to a minimum.

Of course, there is option d). Just say NO! to the extra work.

If you can afford to do this, you might send the enquirer along to me.

26 Teaching

26·1 Introduction

I had been turning professionally for a good twelve years before I decided to start teaching.

I had trained people who wanted to work for me of course, but I had been paying them. Whilst that certainly was teaching, it was not like the teaching which I got into. For the student to pay me was a big responsibility.

26·2 Early Days

My first student actually came into the workshop to read the electricity meter.

He watched whatever it was I was doing on the lathe and then when I had finished, asked me to do another one.

The meter was forgotten. Some twenty minutes later, he said "I've got a lathe in the garage at home and I'm frightened of it".

I said, "You've just overcome the biggest problem you'll ever have with the lathe. You've admitted you're frightened of it".

He ended up by coming out to me on regular two-hourly visits each week, and we both learned a lot.

At that time I couldn't really take on more than one student at a time, due to workshop space – or the lack of it – and that was a good thing.

I learned to think ahead of my student, helping him first of all to avert disasters and then to recognize the danger signals on his own.

26·3 How Many?

My own preference is still to teach on a one-to-one basis, but two students at a time is the norm.

I have been responsible for up to five at a time, and that in a strange workshop, on strange machines and with strange – and blunt – tools.

Happily, one or two of the students are usually my own and I know that they can be left safely for some time without them doing anything irreparable.

I have occasionally found a student who didn't like being watched. That is like finding a fencing master who doesn't like being hit.

When I find such a woodturning student, then 'a couple of minutes' demonstration and let him get on with it, is the order of the day, but I try to position myself somewhere in the workshop where I can actually watch him from a distance.

The ability to detect problems by sound is a distinct advantage as well. If I am working with one student and I can hear that all is not well with the other one, I can intervene before disaster strikes. Or before anything else strikes, come to that.

26·4 Aids to Teaching

I like each student to have a firm idea of what they are trying to achieve, be it a roughing cut, a planing cut with a skew chisel, production of a rolling pin, a lidded box, a waney edge bowl or whatever. An example or at the very least a drawing of what they are making should be close at hand if possible.

To put over my meaning, I usually use pencil and paper and at the end of each session, the student takes away the sketches as an aide-memoire.

27 Questions and Answers

I asked a number of people, either potential, existing or ex students, to give me up to ten questions each, the object being to get an idea of the worries which newcomers to the craft have.

Some of the questions were duplicated, some irrelevant, but all genuine.

Are there recommended turning speeds for different types of wood?

It is largely the size rather than the type of wood which determines lathe speed. Large diameter = slow speed, small diameter = high speed.

However, I have found that the softer, more open-grained timbers give better results at a higher speed.

Depending upon the length of wood, type of tool being used, whether I have an audience or not, I usually turn anything up to 2″ square at 2,000 r.p.m.

Is there any application where a tailstock fixed centre is preferable to a live centre?

At the tailstock end of the lathe, extra capacity between centres can be found by using the short fixed centre instead of the live centre. This is the only advantage which I can think of.

However, fixed centres can be used in the headstock.

See chapter 9 for more details.

Is it possible to turn a bowl satisfactorily, when a bowl gouge is not available?

Flat top bowls can be produced using scrapers alone, but better results can be obtained quicker using a gouge for most, if not all of the work.

Some spindle gouges can be used to hollow out the inside of smaller bowls, but it is better to invest in the real thing rather than to have a gouge which has to be re-ground specially for bowls.

Handle length is also a prime consideration, the long-handled bowl gouge giving greater control.

What woods are not suitable for turning for a beginner?

It is probably better to ask what timbers are suitable, and this is usually dictated by availability.

Beech and ramin were the timbers which I did most of my initial professional learning on, each being available from local saw mills in those days.

I soon learned to avoid afrormosia and iroko because of their abrasive qualities on the tools and also their effect on my health. Afrormosia I dubbed 'sneeze wood' and iroko became 'headache wood'.

Oak is also an abrasive timber, and can tend to split during turning if not treated with sympathy and respect.

Nowadays there are an amazing variety of timbers available through specialist suppliers. I suggest to any newcomer to the craft, that after they come to terms with good old faithful beech, they try a second timber. But be careful, and watch out for problems. Not only mechanical, but also medical.

What grades of paper are recommended for sanding rotating wood?

Choice of grade depends upon a number of things: Type of timber, finish achieved from tool, ultimate use for product, etc.

As a general guide, I rarely use anything coarser than 100 grit initially, and frequently start with 150.

I did once hear of a distinguished turner who started with 25 grit, but I believe he has since mended his ways. I couldn't help wondering however, if he used the 25 grit to fell the tree in the first place!

What problems are liable to arise when turning laminated wood of differing hardness?

It is not usually the wooden laminations which cause problems, but the glue.

Tool 'bounce' can be a bit of a worry (see chapter 12·5), but keeping the tool sharp, keeping sanding to a minimum to avoid the carry over of sanding dust from dark to light timbers and indeed, the careful preparation work needed beforehand are all to be considered when undertaking this type of timber saving, but labour intensive work.

What are the essential features of a lathe?

See chapter 3.

What are the essential tools?

A roughing gouge, a spindle gouge and a parting tool, but see chapter 4·2.

What would be useful extra tools?

Again, see chapter 4.

What speeds are used when turning?

See the answer to question 1.

What height should a lathe be?

See chapter 3·7.

How do you sharpen tools, i.e., grinding, honing, stropping?

Regarding grinding and honing, see chapter 5. I did experiment with stropping for a while but gave it up as too time-consuming for the results achieved.

What finishes are best for turnery?

This is one of the millions of questions which are easily asked and which could have books written on the answers.

Basically, I use three types of finish, when more than the normal sanded finish is required, that is. (See chapter 13.)

Sanding sealer (so called because it is used in the furniture trade to seal wood prior to sanding in preparation for the finishing process) is used a great deal as the first, and sometimes the only, surface finish.

Sanding sealer is sometimes used in conjunction with paste wax, which is so called because it has a soft, paste-like texture, as opposed to the harder waxes.

Cooking oil is also used, primarily on turnery which is to come into contact with foodstuffs. I have occasionally been asked if the cooking oil ever goes rancid and I can only say that I have had no complaints so far.

Nowadays there are almost as many finishes to choose from as there are timber choices available or tools to work it with.

I have heard of one turner who makes baby rattles and finishes them with baby oil, thus being confident that there should be no compatibility problems when the rattle is chewed.

Experiment, but do it with an open mind.

What is the cause of 'ripple' on the surface of the turned wood?

A smooth disruption to the turned surface of a piece of wood is caused by either the tool moving away from the wood, the wood moving away from the tool, or a combination of both.

This disruption takes the form of either shallow spirals which usually run in the direction of the last cut, or in extreme cases, a 'hammered' finish on the surface of the wood.

If the tool is moving away from the wood, it can be caused by a blunt tool, a loose tool rest, a thin tool which flexes during use, too much tool overhang between tool rest and work, or insufficient control during the cut.

If the wood is moving away from the tool, this can be caused by a blunt tool, worn bearings in head or tailstock, work loose between centres, or a thin piece of work flexing away from the tool due to insufficient support from the free hand. (See chapter 12·2.)

All of these possibilities should be checked for and rectified.

And don't forget, if all else fails, sharpen the tool!

What type of work holding device is the best?

See chapter 9 on chucks.

Does the floor have to be concrete or can I put my lathe on a wooden shed floor?

See chapter 1·1.

Can a lathe be used whilst sitting down?

(This question was asked for medical reasons)

I know of at least one professional turner who works sitting down, but he is a miniaturist.

Generally speaking, a woodturner stands up to the lathe, moving his body, frequently from the ankles up, to control cuts.

However, if there are practical reasons why a sitting position must be adopted, I see no reason why at least a great deal of enjoyment and possibly even a living, can't be had from producing the smaller turnery, such as lace bobbins, boxes etc.

Does it take very long to get used to turning wood on a lathe and are there books with patterns of simple things to make?

I am learning all the time and made some horrendous mistakes when I first started turning.

Nowadays however, there are so many sources of basic instruction available in the form of books, demonstrations, courses of instruction and videos, that no-one should have to go through the hazardous learning ordeal that I, and many like me, endured and survived.

There are a number of books with lathe projects in them. The bibliography of this book gives some of them. Also look for inspiration in books on treen, visits to museums etc.

When buying a second-hand lathe, what would you look for?

The reason why it is being sold!

Some lathes nowadays are of very poor quality and will find their way on to the second hand market very quickly, their owners realising too late that they made a poor investment.

Of the home-produced lathes, most are good, the well-established names such as Arundel, Coronet, Harrison, Myford and Tyme usually being good buys.

But ask around amongst other turners, read magazines, do what I did in 1966 and look at magazines to see which lathes the professional turners/writers use.

If you visit a trade show and see a lathe which is not being demonstrated, ask yourself why.

There are enough professional turners around nowadays, for one of them to be found who is willing to be associated with a particular lathe, if it is a good one.

See also chapter 3·6.

What are the most common accidents?
(This question was from one of my fencing students who is now taking an active interest in turning.)

Apart from the occasional cuts, abrasions and outbreaks of hammer rash which most hand workers are liable to suffer from time to time, I have only twice needed some minor medical attention due to punctures.

On both occasions the punctures were a result of my own inattention when using saws. (See chapter 20.)

The hand turning lathe is one of only two machines which I have in my workshop, and which, if I employed people I wouldn't have to constantly supervise.

The second machine is the pillar drill.

If someone is determined to have an accident, then no machine is safe from them. If common sense prevails, then there should be no mishaps.

Bibliography

The following list shows just a few of the many books on turning available today.

It is by no means a complete list, nor can it be truly up to date, as new titles are appearing all the time.

My advice to the newcomer is as it has always been – read just *one* of the books on turning which start with the basics. Most newcomers to the craft avidly read all they can lay their hands upon – a lot of the advice which they thereby soak up being contradictory.

Reading just one book and using the methods suggested by the author will be far less confusing than trying too many styles too soon.

Authors like Frank Pain and Peter Child are hard to beat in this field, although they are both now out of date regarding work holding methods.

Once the basic skills have been acquired, then the turner can develop his or her own style.

BOULTER, Bruce
Woodturning in Pictures, London, Bell & Hyman (1983) 0 237 456893

CHILD, Peter
The Craftsman Woodturner, 2nd revised edition. London, Unwin Hyman (1987) 0 044401175, paperback.

KEY, Ray
Woodturning and Design, London, Batsford (1986) 0 7134 41151 (to be reprinted late 1988)

PAIN, Frank
The Practical Woodturner, London, Bell & Hyman (1983) 0 7135 1423 X, paperback

PETERS, Geoff
Woodturning, London, Arco (1961). Out of print

RAFFAN, Richard
Turning Wood, London, Bell & Hyman (1986) 0 7135 26963, paperback
Newtown, Connecticut, Taunton Press (1985) 0 918804248, paperback

SAINSBURY, John
The Craft of Woodturning, New York, Sterling (1984) 0 8069 78287, paperback

STURT, George
The Wheelwright's Shop, Cambridge, CUP (1923) 0521 091950, paperback